Understanding

SHAME

Why It Hurts,
How It Helps,
How You Can Use It to
Transform Your Life

Understanding SHAME

Why It Hurts, How It Helps, How You Can Use It to Transform Your Life

By Eunice Cavanaugh, M.Ed., M.S.W.
Edited by Pamela Espeland

JOHNSON ⬡ INSTITUTE
Minneapolis 1989

Published by the Johnson Institute
7151 Metro Blvd. Suite 250
Minneapolis MN 55435

Library of Congress Cataloging-in-Publication Data

Cavanaugh, Eunice.
  Understanding shame.

  1. Shame. I. Espeland, Pamela. II. Title.
BF575.S45C38 1989   152.4   89-19837
ISBN 0-935908-50-1

DEDICATION

To Wanda, Bonnie, Cindy, Bill, and all my other teachers

ACKNOWLEDGMENTS

Over the past several years of clarifying my understanding of shame, both the significance and dimensions of shame have awed and dazzled me. The more I have studied, the more clients and friends have shared with me, the more I have observed the subtle and not-so-subtle manifestations of shame within myself and others, the more deeply I have come to believe that shame truly is the most important and most human of emotions.

At first I viewed shame as a barrier to be eliminated—the immobilizing pain was so apparent. Now I see shame as a human quality to be celebrated. This changing point of view has been the result of a fascinating personal and professional journey.

My journey could not have taken place without the many people who have shared with me their own shame and transformation, as well as the pain that can indeed be a barrier to healing. My journey could not have happened without the patience of others who have walked beside me, giving me acceptance when they had no understanding — in fact, when they thought I had lost track of the path completely.

As I approached the decision of whom to name in the Acknowledgments section of this book, it quickly became apparent that I owe a debt of gratitude to many, many people. Because I came to the helping profession later in my life, much of my early learning came from an astounding array of people who consider themselves "ordinary" but are, in fact, most extraordinary in the personal gifts they possess and in their ability to share their gifts with unconditional generosity. As you pick up this book, hoping for a map for your own journey, my dream for you is that you, too, can find such extraordinary people in your life — that you, too, can give to others of your own gifts.

So instead of a page filled with a list of people who have contributed so richly to my learning, I am thanking you all here. May you be blessed with the grace to recognize your gifts to me.

A special thanks to my editor, Pamela Espeland, and gentle nudger, Carole Remboldt, who have made it possible to bring this particular dream to fruition.

But most of all, I thank my children, whose love for me has been so unconditional and so generous that there is no way for me to express to them or have them understand what a gift they have given me. They believed in me. I am grateful.

Eunice Cavanaugh
September, 1989

CONTENTS

PART II: THE SHAME-ANXIETY CYCLE

INTRODUCTION

James worked hard at his job. He put in extra hours and impressed everyone with his conscientiousness, motivation, and shy, pleasant manner. Yet when he received his first promotion, he was surprised. And when he was promoted again and again, he began feeling deep discomfort and doubt. He became acutely aware of each minor imperfection in his performance. He was convinced that he "didn't deserve" the promotions, pay raises, and respect shown to him by the company and his coworkers. He worried more and more about what was "really" going on. Eventually he became so anxious and depressed that he was hospitalized in a mental health unit. His belief that he was undeserving of the good things in life was so strong that he could no longer function in a world that didn't reflect his view of himself.

Karen could have been pleased and proud to learn that she had been chosen Student of the Month from the Senior Class. Instead, her first thought was, "They must have made a mistake. I don't really deserve this."

Kevin met Sarah at an office party. She was obviously attracted to him. After they had dated for several months, it became clear that Sarah loved him with her whole heart. Kevin was filled with doubt. "What's she after?" he wondered. "No one as gorgeous as Sarah would be interested in me unless there was something in it for her!"

These are real stories about real people I have seen in my counseling practice. And they all illustrate a theme central to this book: *When we believe that we don't deserve the good things in life, our ability to enjoy life is diminished.* This belief robs us of the satisfaction of achievement, the joy of relationships, and the sense of harmony with others and our world. It diminishes the thrill of receiving a gift and the richness of accepting love freely offered. It interferes with our capacity to feel contented and at peace.

Sometimes the I-don't-deserve feeling becomes distorted into the belief that we do deserve the uncomfortable and even terrible things that happen to us.

Randy had a lot of time to himself during his teenage years. His parents left him virtually alone as they pursued their own interests. His mother would shout a string of orders at him as she ran out the door to a committee meeting. His father was coldly contemptuous toward him because he was "uncoordinated." With parents who failed to act like parents, Randy became convinced that he deserved to be ignored and treated badly.

Alice grew up in a happy family where children were loved and valued. Yet when trouble struck later in life, her sense of self-worth foundered. In a single year, her mother underwent a mastectomy, her unmarried daughter became pregnant, her husband underwent quadruple cardiac bypass surgery, and her son was jailed on a DWI (driving while intoxicated) charge. Alice's response was to wonder why she was being "punished." There must be something wrong with her for all of those terrible things to happen!

Carla's best friend was her cousin Mark. From early childhood, they spent a great deal of time together, and Carla often confided in him. When she was raped by this man she had cared about and trusted for so long, she immediately blamed herself. "I should have known better than to be alone with him," she told herself. She believed she deserved what happened.

When we believe that we deserve the bad things in life, we accept misfortune and abuse as an inevitable part of our lives. We accept sarcasm, put-downs, and belittling remarks without protest. People take unfair advantage of us because we believe we don't have the right to defend ourselves. We are exploited and used.

It's important to understand that these beliefs — that we don't deserve good and do deserve bad — can happen to anyone. We all have occasion to doubt ourselves. We all have times when we question our self-worth. Each of us, at some level of awareness, knows that we could often do better at our jobs and our relationships. We all make mistakes. But we don't usually give up on ourselves when we do. Instead, we assess ourselves honestly, reflecting on our behaviors and attitudes to determine our course of action. We talk with people we trust, seeking their advice and opinions. We consider whether and how we should change. If we decide that change is necessary or desirable, we adjust the ways we are thinking and acting. And then we get on with our lives.

For some of us, choosing to change is more difficult. Our personal discomfort may grow so strong, and the pain of self-awareness so intense, that we become paralyzed with hopelessness. We despair that things can ever be different. We play and replay the same scenes of feeling unworthy, isolated, unloved. We endure lives of discouragement and emotional pain, lives that fit Thoreau's description of "quiet desperation."

What makes the difference between hope and hopelessness? From my years of counseling, I believe it is the presence of shame — the deep-down-inside feeling that one is unworthy, unvalued, defective, unlovable. This feeling is difficult to identify or describe. We may be unaware of its impact on our lives because it seems "natural" to us, and because the very nature of shame calls for secrecy and hiding.

One of the strongest indicators of shame in our lives is the feeling that we are unlovable. Here is what psychiatrist Leon Wurmser says about this in his book, *The Mask of Shame*:

> In a sense, love at its peak means being as fully accepted as is humanly possible in the wish for enriching self-expression and in the desire to be gloriously and abidingly fascinated and impressed — and to have reciprocity in this on uncounted levels of communication and attentiveness. Shame is the defeat of such love — the dark side of the night compared with the shining brilliance of this greatest and most creative power.

All of us experience to some degree the struggle between shame and love. It's part of being human. But when love is defeated by shame, the consequences can be tragic. We may lose the capacity "for enriching self-expression" — whether in a creative, artistic sense, or in our desire to feel connected with others and loved by them. Our "ability to be fascinated and impressed" is replaced by a sense of emptiness, and we no longer stand in wonder before life's spectrum of beauty and ugliness. Convinced that we don't deserve offers of friendship and love, we can't accept them. We reject anyone who seeks connection with us.

A word of caution is appropriate here. You may want to read this book very slowly, especially if you have ever experienced strong, debilitating shame. One of the ways we protect ourselves from shame is by covering it up. Uncovering it can cause enormous emotional distress. It's not easy to confront our own isolation, disconnectedness, and emptiness. In fact, it can be downright miserable!

The most effective way to free ourselves from the constricting, frightening belief that we don't deserve good (or do deserve bad) is by facing our shame and learning to understand it.

Then we can start opening the doors and windows of our being to the possibilities of a new beginning. Then we can put aside the fear that life is an endurance contest without meaning or hope, and begin exploring the endless joys of loving and being loved.

3

PART I:

SHAME, GUILT, ANGER, AND THE SELF

CHAPTER ONE

SHAME AND GUILT

The Positive Power of Shame

"You ought to be ashamed of yourself!" Most of us can remember a time when we heard or said these words. We cringed in embarrassment, mortification, and anger — all dismaying expressions of shame.

Shame is often connected to feeling intensely uncomfortable feelings. We squirm in the present awareness of shame. We are reminded of times we don't want to remember. Because of that, we generally consider shame to be bad. We focus on how shame hurts, and we often misunderstand how shame can help us to become more self-creating, self-nurturing, self-directing.

Shame can tell us when our behaviors or thoughts are not in harmony with what we know to be right, moral, or true. Shame is a call from our inner selves to transform ourselves — or, as psychoanalyst Helen Merrell Lynd explained, "to become a revelation of oneself, of one's society, and of the human condition." Other authorities see shame as the most human of our attributes, and one of the most important.

Shame can be a driving force for an internal moral and ethical debate that leads to change. As such, shame can be a positive power in our lives.

By helping us to be self-regulating, self-nurturing, and self-directing, shame enables us to know ourselves better and reach our full potential.

Shame-Based Identity

For some of us, however, shame can be so undermining and paralyzing that we develop a shame-based identity — a devastated sense of self. To be shame-based is to have a fundamental belief that we are unlovable, defective, worthless, "less than."

Our capacity to feel shame then distorts our perceptions and defeats our lives. Extreme shame-based beliefs limit our ability to love, to trust, to form relationships, and to govern our own behaviors. They prevent us from achieving harmony within ourselves, our families, our communities, and with God. They convince us that we don't deserve the good things in life, or that we deserve the bad.

Our shame response can be like quicksand. On the surface, our ability to feel shame appears to be natural or predictable. As the surface of the quicksand conceals a dangerous mix of unstable sand and water, so, too, the natural appearance of shame can disguise an unstable emotional condition of secrecy and confusion.

Like quicksand, the unstable emotional condition can be treacherous and destructive. But we can learn how to avoid entrapment or save ourselves if we fall in unaware.

The Mask of Guilt
and the Differences
Between Shame and Guilt

Because shame is such an intense and painful feeling, it is often masked or camouflaged by other emotions. One major masking emotion is guilt.

The words guilt and shame are frequently used together or as synonyms. In fact, they are very different — not only in the way they reveal themselves, but also in the way we experience them. And they have very different consequences in our lives.

Guilt is about what we do. Shame is about who we are, a much deeper level of feeling. Unconsciously, we face the lesser of the two uncomfortable feelings.

Elliott talked about a time when he found himself annoyed because there was no clerk to assist him as he shopped for a greeting card. "I'm just going to take this card and walk out!" he exclaimed to himself. "But that would be shoplifting," he thought guiltily. Only later was he aware of his shame. He blushed, saying, "I can't believe that I'm the kind of person who would even consider taking something out of a shop without paying for it."

A compulsive BINGO player, **Marty** grinned ruefully as she became aware of how she had unconsciously played up her guilt when her husband confronted her about her losses. "Okay!" she would say to him. "So I lost again. What do you want me to do, get down on my knees and apologize? I know I shouldn't have done it!" She had used her guilt to mask the shame she felt about her excessive BINGO playing.

Experiences

We experience guilt when our thoughts or actions are contrary to our own (or society's) codes, standards, or moral guidelines. Guilt is verbalized as "I have done something bad." Physically, it is a cringing sensation, a lifting of the head as though looking toward a source of punishment.

We talk about having a "guilty conscience," an "inner voice" which prompts us to reveal our transgressions — like the child who goes to the parent and says, "I'm sorry. I really did see the rock that broke the lawnmower blade. I just didn't stop to move it out of the way." Guilt is behind the newspaper stories we read about people who return books to the library after many years, or send money to a former employer to pay for a petty theft committed long ago.

We experience shame when we fall short of our own (or someone else's) expectations of what we ought to be. If we were to verbalize shame, we might say, "I am bad." Physically, it is evidenced by blushing, covering the face, shrinking into oneself. We feel exposed, as if we have been caught with our pants down. We want to disappear.

Another dimension to shame is the sensation of transparency. As one of my clients said, "It feels as though everyone can see my shame right here on my forehead." Another said, "It feels like I'm sitting in church and everybody can tell by looking at me that I had sex with my daughter." There is a quality of helplessness tied to the sense of transparency.

With guilt, we can choose to reveal our transgression or keep it hidden. With shame, we feel compelled to cover it up. Yet there is always the sense that others can see right through us.

Consequences

The consequences of guilt are very different from the consequences of shame. This is a critical distinction.

With guilt, we can apologize, confess, make amends for violating particular codes, standards, or guidelines, and get on with our lives. For example: We drive through a stoplight without pausing. We realize our error, thinking, "I have done a bad thing." We feel guilty. Maybe we are caught and given a ticket symbolic of our breaking the law, in which case we pay the fine (make amends) and that's that. We probably feel some regret about the money we have to spend, but we learn from the experience to stop at stoplights in the future.

With shame, the belief that "I am bad" can trap us in a mire of helplessness and hopelessness. For example: We run the stoplight, realize our error, and think, "I'm so awful because I've broken the law!" Or, "I'm so stupid!" Even if we are caught, given a ticket, and pay the fine (make amends), we still feel defective and "less than." We feel exposed to the officer who stops us and to the people who drive by and stare. Our shame-based identity defines us as a worthless citizen.

Often, guilt and shame can occur simultaneously. For example: We run the light. We feel guilty — "I have done a bad thing." At the same time, we are swamped by shame — "I'm so awful because I've broken the law." Because shame affects us at a deeper level of feeling, the tendency is to quickly conceal it behind the mask of guilt. It is always more comfortable to feel guilty than to feel ashamed.

If we are simultaneously feeling guilt and shame, it is far safer for us to reveal our guilt than to allow ourselves or others to see our shame.

Andy's fingers were wet as he carried the plastic-coated box of chicken through the kitchen of the fast-food restaurant where he had worked for two weeks. Andy dropped the box, spilling ten pounds of chicken across the dirty floor. He was deeply embarrassed as well as fearful for his job. As he quickly scooped the chicken pieces back into the box, knowing full well that they would have to be thrown out, his shame-based self-talk went something like this: "You did it again, you dumbhead! Always screwing up! How do you expect to ever hold a decent job when you're such an idiot?" He felt worthless, defective, exposed as a klutz. Then his supervisor rounded the corner. "What's going on here?" he asked. Andy immediately responded, "I dropped the chicken. I don't know why they coat these boxes with plastic. Anyone ought to know that they're going to be slippery."

What happened here? Andy's shame was quickly masked by guilt, which he was able to acknowledge to himself and his supervisor. The presence of shame was unacknowledged and covered even deeper by his defensiveness.

Words and Wordlessness

Another difference between shame and guilt has to do with the way we become conscious of each. Guilt seems to be attached to words. We can verbalize what is happening and what we are feeling. Herbert Morris, editor of a collection of writings about guilt and shame, uses the term "auditory images" to describe this sensation. We can hear the words that are part of the guilt experience.

Have you ever seen a comedy sketch where the comedian commits some wrongdoing? A deep, booming voice comes out of the upper reaches saying, "Now you've done it!" Much the same situation happens when we are guilty of a violation. Our inner voice says, "Uh-oh! You're in trouble now!"

Shame, on the other hand, seems to be pre-verbal (before words) or nonverbal (without words). Shame tends to be accompanied by "visual images," pictures or sensations that are not connected to language. This explains why, when we are feeling shame, we are virtually speechless! We simply can't find the words to express this feeling to ourselves or others.

For example, we go to the podium to accept our Student-of-the-Month award and "forget" our carefully rehearsed acceptance speech as we become aware of all the people. We feel exposed, vulnerable — and ashamed — even at the same time we are proud of the award. We have a visual image. We "see" all the eyes upon us. We can't access the memorized words, so we are silent or perhaps mumble something — anything — and stumble from the stage.

One of my clients repeatedly uses the phrase, "I don't have any words," as she relives deeply shaming memories during her counseling sessions.

This wordless state has a profound impact. For adults, it creates a sense of being out of control. One of the physical manifestations of shame is a blank, unseeing stare — a sign of sheer panic.

Without words, we cannot express our shame. We want to let it out, but we also want to hide it and keep it secret. The secrecy stimulates more shame. We feel more anxious and out of control. The rapidity with which this happens also contributes to our wordless state. It's the emotional equivalent of having the rug jerked out from under us.

Harold had reached a point in his therapy where he felt ready to go to a group where the focus would be on family healing. As he talked about the experience later, he said, "I was totally unprepared for how quickly I fell apart. As we got into a role-play, I began to feel slightly uneasy because one of the women reminded me of my mother. As she began to act out her anger, I had a terrible flashback. Suddenly I was incapable of telling the others how afraid I was. I just sat there, trapped inside my old shame. I was totally speechless. I could feel myself gasping for air, trying to speak on my own behalf, but words wouldn't come."

Limits and Boundaries

Still another difference between shame and guilt has to do with limits and boundaries. Guilt is self-contained; we feel only *our own* guilt. Shame, in contrast, is without limits or boundaries. We can feel shame for ourselves, for others, even for our entire race or culture.

Jake co-led a treatment group for adults who had been sexually abused as children by their fathers or other males. As he related how difficult it was to listen to their stories, he said, "Sometimes I leave the sessions feeling ashamed that I am a man."

11

Jake didn't feel guilt. He wasn't guilty of abuse. He did, however, feel shame for his gender — for other males.

In our everyday conversations, we often hear people say, "I felt so embarrassed for them!" Hardly anyone ever says, "I felt so guilty for them."

Labeling Feelings

To further complicate our understanding of shame and guilt, we tend to label them both as "bad" feelings. We usually do this unconsciously.

Trish sat sobbing in her chair, which she had pushed back into the farthest corner of my office as if to take refuge there. "I'm so happy!" she told me. "Things are going really great for me now. I just thought I'd drop by to talk about old times and let you know that Lyle and I are very happy together." When I pointed out the discrepancy between what she was saying and how she was acting, she became very angry. "Well, I am happy!" she insisted. We've been married six weeks now. Lyle is wonderful to me. And . . . ." She burst into another torrent of sobs. As we explored the contradiction between her words and feelings, she began talking about how marriage was triggering a lot of shameful feelings and flashbacks to her abusive childhood. At the same time, she "knew" that new brides are supposed to be happy. Trish was convinced that it was "good" to feel happy and "bad" to feel the old shame and anger stirring in her again.

In fact, feelings are neither "good" nor "bad." Feelings just are. To label them can be confusing and crazy-making.

Shame and guilt are neither "good" nor "bad." They just are. They may feel uncomfortable, but they serve a purpose in our lives: They carry messages to us about ourselves and our environment. If we didn't feel shame and guilt, what would keep us from behaving shamelessly and guiltlessly?

Individuals who seem incapable of feeling shame and guilt are judged by society to be antisocial, amoral, even psychopathic. Their behavior falls outside acceptable standards. They do not self-correct. They are shameless, and the damage they inflict upon others and society is truly shameful.

The Value of Shame and Guilt

Psychoanalyst Gerhard Piers described shame and guilt as possibly "the most important feelings." While he acknowledged that too much shame and guilt can harm us, Piers concluded that both are necessary to the healthy development of our sense of self, to the formation of character, and to the development of our ability to live cooperatively in society.

Shame and guilt are affirmations of our humanness. They guide us in our quest for a more satisfying way to live.

CHAPTER TWO

SHAME AND ANGER

The Mask of Anger

Like guilt, anger can serve to mask or camouflage shame. It can occur simultaneously with shame to protect us from the pain of feeling exposed as worthless and unlovable. It is more comfortable to feel angry than to feel ashamed.

While anger may occur by itself as a response to some external threat or internal trigger, many psychotherapists believe that anger is more often a secondary feeling. It shields us from the unpleasantness of a primary feeling, one we experience first in response to a situation or event. Generally, the primary feeling is fear, inadequacy, helplessness, or anxiety, any of which can be closely tied to shame.

Consider the father whose daughter has run into the street in front of an oncoming car. Fearful that his precious child is about to be hurt or even killed, the father calls to her, darts out to grab her, holds her close — and spanks her! "Don't you ever do that again!" he says sharply. "Don't you know you could get hurt?" The father's anger rises quickly to shield him from his primary feeling of fear. Very seldom will a parent in this situation hold a child close and say gently, "I was so very, very afraid you would be hurt!"

Or consider a time when you were feeling inadequate or confused. Maybe it was when you were trying to hook up your latest high-tech purchase. Reading the garbled instructions, you struggled to fit the widget to the whatsis. You studied the instructions one more time. The illustration, you noticed, didn't show clearly which side was the front and which was the back. Nor did it indicate whether the widget would break if you pushed too hard to snap it into the whatsis.

You probably started thinking to yourself, "Thousands of these things have been sold. Why can't I get mine together?" Rather than feel inadequate, you got angry. You may have thrown the widget across the room and stormed out to the kitchen for another cup of coffee.

There seems to be a close correlation between the intensity of anger and the intensity of the shame it masks. The more our feelings are based on shame, the more frequently and fiercely we get angry. Or we might "numb out" and detach from our feelings altogether, depending on how skilled we are at using denial or minimization. (*Denial* is the refusal to accept a powerful reality; *minimization* is the attempt to make a powerful reality less serious than it really is.)

Whether expressed (acted out or verbalized) or repressed (pushed down or stuffed), the shame-anger connection is a powerful one.

Physical Consequences of Shame

Shame affects more than our emotions. It also has physical consequences that occur so quickly and feel so awful it's little wonder we choose anger over shame.

> **Sally** was sitting with a group of people she had met the day before at her church's annual campout. As they relaxed around the glowing campfire, the talk flowed easily. There was a warm sense of camaraderie as everyone enjoyed the fellowship. Sally thought of a joke she had heard recently. She offered to tell it and was given the floor. Enjoying the attention, she told her little story well, got to the punchline — and couldn't remember it! Immediately she blushed and broke out in a cold sweat. She wanted to curl up and hide. She felt as though she was being pulled down into a cold swamp. She wished she could just disappear instead of being exposed as a "lousy storyteller." Then, all at once, the anger came. Charged with adrenaline and the fight-or-flight reflex, she said furiously, "Dammit, I can never remember punchlines!" Realizing that she had just made matters worse by swearing in front of people from her church, she felt even more ashamed. She pushed her chair back and stomped off into the night.

For Sally, the heat of anger was preferable to the cold, clammy sense of being swamped by shame. This doesn't mean that she deliberately chose between them; masking shame with guilt or anger is an unconscious act. We don't say to ourselves, "I'm going to get angry (or guilty) now because then I won't feel so exposed and ashamed." Our unconscious mind makes the choice for us.

Anger feels better than shame, but like any mask it isn't the real thing. It interferes with our ability to face ourselves. It keeps us from understanding why we repeat certain behaviors. We may realize that our life isn't the way we want it to be, but we can't perceive the underlying shame-related reasons because they are covered up by anger.

Labeling Anger "Bad" or "Good"

Our society teaches that it's acceptable and even "good" for men to be angry and express their anger. Men who show anger are described as powerful, strong, manly, or macho. In contrast, women who show anger are described as bitchy or shrewish — loaded words implying that anger is a "bad" feeling for women to experience or express.

Early on, many men learn that it's "bad" to feel inadequate, fearful, helpless, or confused and to show these feelings when they have them. Tearful little boys are told, "Come on now, be a big boy and don't cry." Early on, women learn that it's "good" for a woman to feel afraid or sad and to express these uncomfortable feelings through their actions. Tearful little girls are told, "Come here and let me hold you until you feel better."

Men who have been physically, sexually, or psychologically abusive to their wives or partners consistently identify uncomfortable sensations like hurt, disappointment, helplessness, fear, guilt, and shame as underlying their anger. Because these feelings are labeled "unmanly" or "wimpy," this leads to even more anger. Meanwhile, abusive men are often supported in their anger (and violence) by friends who say things like, "Who wouldn't get mad if their wife didn't have supper ready on time?"

For women, the shame-anger connection may be complicated by the belief that anger is "unwomanly." Sensing anger rising in her body, a woman may feel ashamed of being less than a woman "should be" (patient, understanding, and quiet). And suddenly she is caught in an intense cycle: Anger triggers more shame, which triggers more anger, and on and on.

In addition, women receive social messages that encourage them to deny or minimize their anger.

> "My boss always brings urgent letters to be typed thirty minutes before closing time," **Patti** told me. "When I finally expressed my anger, he called me on the carpet and said, 'We don't want any bitchy secretaries around here. Have you noticed how cooperative Jane is when she is asked to work overtime?'"

Labeling anger can be crazy-making. What about the times when our anger leads to violence? How can that be "good"? Or what about the times when someone we love does something that makes us angry? Does feeling angry mean that we are "bad"?

On the other hand, if happiness is "good," are we supposed to be happy constantly, regardless of what goes on in our lives? What about the times when we witness our parents hurting each other verbally or physically? The conflict between what we feel, and what we think we should feel, can have serious consequences. These may range from physical symptoms such as "nervous stomach" or headache to intense levels of anxiety and depression.

> "My mom drives me crazy when she starts telling me how I should feel," **Patti** went on. "I was telling her how mad I get when my boss brings me those letters to type at 4:30. Right away she starts telling me how I should be glad to have such a good job and I should be happy that he hasn't fired me. It's just like when I was a kid. She and Dad would have horrible fights in the mornings after he'd been drinking. Then she'd tell me to 'put on a smile when you go to school. Nobody likes a grump.' I wanted to scream at her then, I want to scream at her now. It brings back all of those old feelings of just wanting to run in front of a truck on the way to school so it would be over."

Anger as a Mask for Joy

Paradoxically, there are times when the primary feeling underlying anger can be happiness, joy, or some other positive emotion.

Why would feeling happy make us angry? Perhaps because we believe that we don't deserve to be happy; perhaps because our happiness makes us feel too revealed or exposed. When we are happy, we let down our guard emotionally. We show that we care about someone or something, and this reveals an area where we are vulnerable. Our sense of exposure is followed by shame and immediately masked by anger.

It's risky to let others know what makes us happy, especially if we are involved with abusive persons.

> **Adam** learned early in life that the only way to hang onto anything important was to pretend that it didn't matter to him. Otherwise his brother would try to destroy it. "When my team won the flag football championship," Adam told me, "he smashed my trophy. When I started dating, he made fun of my girlfriends."

Adam's response was to get angry at himself for letting down his guard around his brother.

When we believe that we don't deserve good, anger can rise up to cover our joy at experiencing or receiving it. This anger has an almost superstitious quality to it. We often hear people say things like, "Sure, this promotion is just to set me up so that when I'm laid off, I'll be even more disappointed!" To the shame-based person, having something good happen is a challenge to their belief system: "Why would my boss promote me now? She must be after something."

Anger as a Mask for Dependence

Anger can rise to our defense in yet another way: to mask the feelings of helplessness and inadequacy that stem from being dependent on others.

When we think of being dependent, we usually think of children. Children are totally dependent. Their lives, even their sense of who they are, depend on someone else meeting their needs. If their needs are not met, they will die. This applies to more than the obvious physical needs for food, clothing, and shelter: Children whose emotional needs aren't met are also at risk of death.

You may already have heard of the famous study from the early 1900's. In some foundling hospitals of the time, the infant mortality rate was virtually 100 percent. When researchers set out to discover the cause, they quickly identified other hospitals where children were not dying — in fact, they seemed to thrive! As the researchers examined the medical possibilities, they learned why these infants were doing so well: The staff took time to cuddle and hug them, rocking them and holding them close. In the hospitals with high death rates, the infants received the same nutrition and the same general care of their bodily needs, but no one touched them or met their emotional needs. Out of that research came a prescription for TLC (tender loving care) to be given to hospitalized infants on a regular basis.

You've probably seen the bumper stickers that ask, "Have you hugged your kid today?" These affirm children's need for emotional nurturance. You also may have seen the spin-offs: "Have you hugged your horse?" — or your dog, or your cat? Strangely, there don't seem to be any that ask, "Have you hugged your friend?" — or your sweetie or spouse. Too often, we adults ignore our own need for connectedness, or we pretend that we've outgrown it. We deny or minimize our dependence on others.

We all have dependence needs, regardless of our age. We are all social creatures. We are conceived out of union and seek union with others throughout our lives. We depend on cooperation with others to meet our physical and emotional needs. And further, as psychiatrist Leon Wurmser points out, to meet our desire for love — to be as fully accepted as humanly possible.

How much we need others depends on our emotional, physical, intellectual, or spiritual condition. At times we manage very nicely on our own. At other times — when we are ill, for example — we may need or want help. At still other times we have a reserve of energy that enables us to do the helping.

This balance of sharing, giving, and receiving can be seriously impaired if we operate from a shame-based identity.

19

Abandonment Anxiety

A shame-based identity makes it difficult to satisfy our dependence needs. We feel exposed as unlovable, defective, worthless, "less than" if we reveal our need for others. Our sense of exposure can lead in turn to profound anxiety and debilitating fear.

Anxiety rooted in shame reduces us to an emotional state of helplessness similar to that of a child who is not being cared for and is at risk of death. This terrifying sensation has been aptly named *abandonment anxiety*, or fear of abandonment. For an infant to be abandoned, emotionally or physically, is to face the very real possibility of death. An adult experiencing abandonment anxiety feels the same fear that an infant feels.

For adults whose childhood needs were met minimally or inconsistently, almost any occasion of shame can trigger abandonment anxiety. This is what happened to Sally when she couldn't remember the punchline of her story. In her words, she felt as though she were "being pulled down into a cold swamp." Other clients have described it as a feeling of being submerged, swallowed up, or overwhelmed.

Our bodies and minds move quickly to protect us from this horrible feeling. Anger rises to warm us, to increase our oxygen intake when our breathing is strained by the onslaught of shame. The more intense our fear of abandonment, the more intense our anger, even to the point of rage.

Dependence Rage

The term *dependence rage* has been coined to describe the extreme anger which masks exposure of our dependence needs.

Picture an infant who feels the first pangs of hunger and fusses briefly. As his hunger increases, he cries more loudly to alert his nursing mother to this critical need. For some reason his mother doesn't respond immediately, and the infant's demands increase. When the mother finally picks up the baby and puts him to her breast, he's so furious that he bites her! This is dependence rage.

JoAnne and Peter have agreed to meet at their favorite restaurant for dinner. Peter arrives a little early because he is so eager to spend this time with Joanne, who is not yet there. He waits patiently for a few moments, then begins to worry, "Did I get the time wrong? Has she forgotten?" A few more moments pass and he becomes increasingly anxious. He starts wondering if she has had car trouble — or maybe an accident! "What if she's been hurt?" he frets. "What if she's dying? What would I do without her?" When JoAnne walks in 17 minutes late, Peter jumps up from his chair and says accusingly, "Where have you been? Do you realize how long you've made me wait?"

This is dependence rage, brought on by Peter's fear of abandonment. Having suddenly realized that he can't live without Joanne, he feels vulnerable and exposed.

Marea, sexually abused by her father as a child, talks about her mother. "Where was she when Daddy was hurting me?" she shouts. "Why didn't she protect me? Why didn't she stop him from doing those terrible things to me?" Her body shakes as she is swept back to that terrifying period in her past.

This is dependence rage. Marea's need to be loved by her father hadn't been met. Nor had her need to be protected from her father. Instead, her mother had abandoned her to the sexual abuse. Years later, she still felt unlovable, defective, and profoundly angry at her mother.

The Value of Shame and Anger

As we have seen, anger often protects us from our underlying, more uncomfortable shame response. As you become aware of the relationship between anger and shame, you can use your anger as a sign that something is going on in your life that bears deeper exploration. You may be feeling shame. Acknowledging shame is an important step in dealing more effectively with the reality of our pain.

CHAPTER THREE

SHAME AND THE SELF

Toward a Common Language

Each of us is born with a "person-ality," a "self" that is separate and distinct from others. "Self"-awareness begins at birth, a time when we have no words to express our "selves." It is such an elementary part of our being that we seldom try to use words to describe our "self."

To understand shame and its place in our lives, however, it is helpful to have a common language, a vocabulary about the self. One way to arrive at such a language is by considering some characteristics of selfness that all people share.

This illustration gives us a place to start.

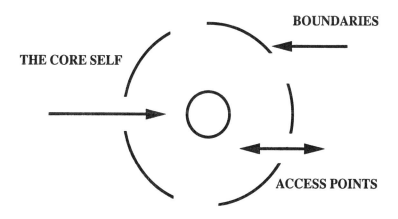

- The *core self* has the potential to be self-creating and self-directing.
- *Boundaries* are the dividing lines between the self and others.
- *Access points* allow us to send and receive information and messages. Through our access points, we can reach out to others, and others can reach in to us. For the self to be healthy, it is essential for this contact to be a matter of choice, with the core self deciding what the boundaries are, when they will open, and who they will open for.

Let's look more closely at these three components of the self.

The Core Self

The core self is hard to describe without sounding mystical or weird. The words used to describe it differ across the disciplines that study what it means to be human — philosophy, theology, psychology, and so forth. Yet they are all attempts to explain the same thing: our capacity to strive for a higher level of development with every part of our being, physical, intellectual, emotional, and spiritual.

From my work with my clients, I have come to see the core self as a "knowing" of good, truth, morality, virtue, rightness. (I use the word "knowing" here to stand for a universal wisdom that transcends externally imposed values. It seems to be within us at birth. It is distinct from what we learn from others.) This knowing recognizes the possibility of achieving harmony with ourselves, our world, our universe; yearns for connectedness; and guides our selves toward that goal.

Psychiatrist Carl Jung believed that we all, deep within us, know how people can be. For example, the image of "mother" (what and how a mother is) appears consistent across cultures. We all have essentially the same ideal image, the same knowing of "mother."

Psychoanalyst Gerhard Piers described a part of the self that has the capacity for the moral and ethical debate that leads to positive change. This part of the self also has the ability to experience shame — the awareness that we are not living up to our own knowing of good, truth, morality, virtue, rightness.

The German word *Funktionlust* can help to explain our urge to realize our potential and guide our selves toward it. Translated, it means the intense desire or lust (not to be taken in a sexual sense) to experience our own "well-functioning." The times when we do — when we succeed in self-directing and live up to our own knowing — are very special times. We call them *peak experiences*, a term coined by Abraham Maslow. It describes the exhilarating feeling we find when we function at the height of our personal best, whether we are using our physical, intellectual, spiritual, or emotional resources.

Thus, the core self seems to contain two critical aspects of our being:

1. the knowing of good, truth, morality, virtue, rightness; and
2. the desire and capacity to self-create, self-direct, and achieve harmony with ourselves, our world, our universe.

Violation of the core self seems to be the source of shame. We violate our own core selves when we perceive ourselves as defective, "less than." Our core selves are violated by others when they treat us as less than we know we are.

Boundaries

Violation of the core self can also occur when we are unable to control the flow of information across our boundaries.

Our boundaries define us as distinct or "disjoined" from others. At birth, we are physically and psychically disjoined from our mothers to become a unique "person-ality." An imaginary dividing line now exists where our self ends and other selves begin.

One way to think of our boundaries is in terms of our "personal space." We've all heard people say things like, "I need my personal space," or "You're crowding my personal space." We can't see, hear, or touch our personal space, but we can feel it, and we accept it as real.

You've probably seen people engaged in conversations where personal space is an important (if unspoken) part of what's going on. One person, intent on making a point, leans over and presses closer; the other shifts or backs away to put more space between them.

What happens when others enter our personal space? That depends on who they are and how they enter. If they are people we care for, we open our boundaries and let them in. We feel comfortable having them close to us. If, on the other hand, they are people we don't care for (or strangers), we feel very uncomfortable if they somehow manage to cross our boundaries and invade our space uninvited.

Access Points

Our access points open to send and receive information and messages. They enable us to reach out to others, and to accept others who reach in to us. They close to limit this back-and-forth flow of information.

The figure on page 23 implies that these access points are fixed and arranged neatly around our boundaries. In fact, they are constantly changing as we allow information to flow inward or outward.

Boundary Violations

When our boundaries are violated, we feel exposed and ashamed. Violations can occur in one of three ways:

1. We unintentionally allow someone access across our boundaries, or
2. Someone forces access across our boundaries, or
3. Our boundaries are opened, leaving our core selves unprotected because we feel shame for someone else.

Let's look more closely at each of these.

Unintentionally Allowed Access

The first type of boundary violation can occur when we are unable to control the output of information. We may be caught unexpectedly in a vulnerable situation. For example, someone walks in on us in the bathroom. Or the minister rings the doorbell as we're screaming at our children. Or our supervisor unexpectedly comes into the shop to find us finishing our last cigarette five minutes after break is over. In each case, others learn something about us that we really don't want them to know.

Strong emotions can lower our inhibitions and cause us to reveal too much of ourselves. In the musical *Chorus Line*, there is a scene in which the characters are being interviewed for positions on the line. As part of the interview, they are asked to talk about their lives and what has brought them to dance and perform in the theater. Judy, a young girl, wants the job badly. With her inhibitions lowered, she begins to talk about the problems she experienced in adolescence as she became aware of boys and sexuality. "Remember practicing kissing with another girl so that when the time came, you'd know how to?" she asks. Looking around her, reading the responses of the others, she suddenly realizes that they didn't practice kissing like that. She feels exposed and flooded with shame. She bends over, curling her body, hiding her face, and slides backward into the shelter of the group. Her physical response symbolizes the closing of her boundaries.

The use of alcohol/other drugs can also lower our inhibitions. Most of the stories we hear about office Christmas parties are really about this side effect of alcohol/other drug use. We have a little too much rum punch, for example, and we tell the boss exactly what we think about the new policy. Later, when we sober up, we feel ashamed.

Forced Access

Forced access, the second type of boundary violation, seems to be critical to the development of a shame-based identity. When someone violates our boundaries by force — physical or emotional — we feel helpless, powerless, out of control, ashamed.

Violations might include insensitive teasing or ridicule, the experience of having others damage or destroy things that are important to us, inappropriate touching, even physical or sexual abuse.

Jan was nine when her family moved to a new city. Coming from a friendly, small-town grade school, she entered a fourth-grade class where the students were very cliquish and status-conscious. Within days of her arrival, she was told she was the only person in the class who lived in a rental home. She was the only one to wear hand-me-down clothes. Her French horn, her classmates told her, "looked like a toilet." But worst of all, Jan said, was when they taunted her on the playground by chanting "Jan, Jan, tin can man." Unable to stop the teasing, alone and helpless, Jan felt ashamed.

Adam was devastated when his brother smashed his championship trophy. Overwhelmed by his brother's greater strength, Adam felt helpless and violated. To make matters worse, his mother ordered him to "quit that crying or I'll give you something you can really cry about!"

Marea shudders as she tells of her father touching her when she was an infant, placing his finger in her vagina as he "taught her how to walk." She knew then that what he was doing was not right, good, or moral. She curls in shame as she describes the helpless infant, powerless to defend herself against the man her core self knew should be the ideal image of "father" — protector and nurturer.

Feeling Shame for Someone Else

The third type of boundary violation can occur when we identify with another person's shame and exposure. This can leave us temporarily "boundaryless" — like the wife who says of her husband, "I was so ashamed to see him walk into the party with his old suit on." Or the child who brings a friend home from school and finds his mother passed out on the couch. He feels personally exposed and ashamed for her.

Marea was surprised to realize that for years she had been feeling shame for her sexually abusive father, not only for herself because of what he had done to her. Her father had violated his own core self by being less than a father should be. When Marea felt shame for her father, she became boundaryless.

Shame as a Signal

Shame leaves us feeling helpless, vulnerable, defective, unlovable. These feelings can be overwhelming and incapacitating. If we look beyond them, however, we can also see that shame is a signal. It alerts us that our core selves may be in danger, that our knowing of good, truth, morality, virtue, rightness may be jeopardized. It tells us that our ability to self-direct may be compromised.

This doesn't explain how we come to believe that we deserve the bad or don't deserve the good. To understand this, we must consider how we interact with others.

CHAPTER FOUR

SHAME AND SELF-CONCEPT

The Core Self and Self-Concept

Our core self — that part of us with the potential to be self-creating and self-directing; the knowing of good, truth, morality, virtue, rightness — seems to be present from birth. Our self-concept — what we believe we are — evolves as we interact with others and our environment. In other words, self-concept is learned.

Psychiatrist Erik Erikson saw a connection between the important caregivers in a child's life and the child's ability to achieve a healthy self-concept. Ideally, Erikson said, adults would convey to the child a "sense of rightful dignity and lawful independence."

If as children we are treated with dignity by our caregivers, we will come to believe that we deserve the good. If as children we are insufficiently nurtured, inadequately cared for, or abused (physically, mentally, or sexually), we will come to believe that we deserve the bad. Part of the paralysis that grips us when we feel intense shame results from the internal conflict of trying to mesh what we know (core self) with what we learn to believe (self-concept).

Marea knew that her father's sexual abuse of her was wrong. She believed that he would not have done it if she deserved to be treated better. But no matter how she tried to accept what happened to her as logical or right, it just didn't make sense. When her believing side proclaimed that she deserved to be treated badly, her knowing self protested. When her knowing side insisted that she didn't deserve such treatment by her father, her believing self suggested that it happened because she deserved it. Marea was mired in confusion and contradiction.

Self-Concept and the Influence of Others

Our self-concept is molded and influenced by the world around us, our parents and siblings, and other important people in our lives. Grandparents, teachers, Scout leaders, spouses, Sunday School teachers — all can affect our self-concept for good or for ill.

Psychiatrist Leon Wurmser says, "Only in seeing and being seen, in hearing and being heard, can we match our self-concept with the concept others have of us." We are blessed if our caregivers mirror our core self's knowing of good, truth, morality, virtue, rightness.

When our caregivers feed us when we're hungry, comfort us when we're unhappy, tend to our different needs for play and sleep, we are supported in our growth by an affirming, nurturing environment. We grow up being respected and therefore capable of respecting ourselves and others. But if we are intensely or consistently disrespected as children, our self-concept can be stunted or damaged.

Four-year-old **Anita** walks up to her deeply depressed mother and asks for something to eat. "Later," her mother replies, apathetic and withdrawn. When Anita asks again, she gets the same answer — "Later." She cautiously asks yet again, but Mother doesn't seem to care that she is hungry! Quietly Anita huddles into the corner of the couch, crying to herself out of hunger and disappointment. Her mother catches a glimpse of her crying and may even struggle to respond, but instead sinks back into the chair and sighs, "Why don't you just get something yourself?"

It's easy to see how Anita will shortly begin to think, "I don't matter to Mother." At four years old, she is not intellectually or emotionally capable of understanding that Mother is sick. So her next thought will likely be, "I don't matter to Mother, so I must be unlovable." Out of this diminished self-concept, shame is born.

The belief that one is unlovable is learned, usually over a period of time. All parents are sometimes unavailable to their children when they are needed. However, children don't usually develop a shame-based self-concept unless they meet with consistent disregard or disaffirmation from caregivers who are emotionally unavailable.

Caregivers may be emotionally unavailable for a number of reasons — depression, alcohol/other drug dependence, rigid notions about appropriate nurturing for children. To a child, however, reasons are irrelevant. What matters is that Mother or Father seems contemptuous or critical, cold or uncaring. We interpret this as meaning, "I don't deserve the good." We feel ashamed of our needs and, ultimately, ashamed of ourselves.

Shame and Self-Concept

In his book *Shame: The Power of Caring* (Cambridge, MA: Schenkman Books, Inc., 1985), Dr. Gershen Kaufman describes shame formation as the failure to build emotional bridges.

Imagine that Person A reaches out to Person B, Person B responds in affirmation. Contact is made; a bridge is created; good feelings result all around.

Now imagine that four-year-old Anita reaches out to her mother, and Mother fails to respond.

If this happens only occasionally, Anita can probably handle it. She is disappointed and feels some emotional pain, but as long as her needs are generally met in a caring fashion, her self-concept is not seriously harmed.

Now imagine that Anita meets with the same response time after time, day after day.

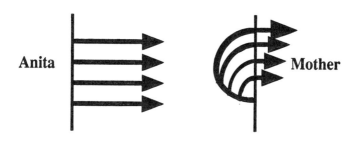

She begins to feel unlovable, worthless, devalued. She starts to believe that she doesn't deserve to be cared for and deserves to be neglected or abused. A healthy self-concept becomes a shame-based identity.

Childhood events that seem insignificant can be critical in the formation of a shame-based identity. "She's our tomboy!" parents say of their daughter, unaware that they are labeling her, setting her apart as different from their ordinary expectations of their daughters. Similarly, a father scornfully says to his son, "Don't be such a sissy!" as the boy is teary-eyed from an injury. Especially if statements such as these indicate that another family member sees the child as different from the rest of the family, the child can experience feelings of isolation and shame.

Shame doesn't have to originate with the family to have a strong and lasting effect. As a character in the musical *Chorus Line* plaintively relates, "One little fart in study hall and they called me 'Stinky' for the next three years!"

Even if we develop a healthy self-concept during childhood, it can crumble later if important persons in our adult lives — spouses, lovers, supervisors — are consistently disaffirming, contemptuous, or critical.

Edie was the envy of all her friends when she left on her honeymoon. Her new husband was a man respected in his career, beloved by the Little Leaguers he coached, and admired by her family. When he slapped her the next morning "because she had misplaced the rental car agreement," Edie was stunned. Later in the day, he explained that he was "just tense" from all the wedding festivities, and she accepted his apology. A month later, he blackened her eye. In her shame, Edie told her friends that she slipped and fell against the corner of the coffee table. As her home life grew worse — her husband criticized her housekeeping, her lovemaking, her taste in clothing — she began to believe that she was somehow "less than" and defective. After all, she thought, she must be or her husband wouldn't treat her the way he did! Like many battered women, Edie became convinced that she deserved to be abused.

An extreme violation of the self — a brutal beating, a rape, or some other form of victimization — can have a devastating effect on our sense of self. Unable to stop the violation, we are flooded with self-doubt and humiliation. We feel small, helpless, and childlike — less than adult, less than deserving of good.

The Personal Experience of Pain

It is important at this point to emphasize that each of us feels pain in uniquely personal ways. What one person handles with apparent ease can be unbearable for another.

Often our experience of pain, and our reaction to it, is based on what has gone before. What may seem like overreaction to a minor incident may be "the last straw" on top of pain from the past. Over and over, I have seen people who were able to deny and minimize the effect of trauma from the past until one last incident pushed them into emotional overload.

> "I'm coming apart at the seams!" **Evie** told me. "I cry at the least provocation. I'm picking fights with my husband. I can't concentrate at work and I'm beginning to fear for my job." She was able to tie her distress to the recent news that her parents were divorcing after many years of an alcoholic marriage. "I know Mom will be okay," she continued. "She supported herself and Dad for years. He's in recovery. I didn't fall apart like this when things were so bad at home. I put myself through college with a part-time job and work-study. I didn't feel like this when my grandmom died. What's happening to me now? My sisters are doing all right!"

It isn't necessary or possible to measure our pain against another person's. When our self-concept has become one of believing that we don't deserve the good, almost anyone else's pain seems greater and more deserving of healing than ours. When our self-concept has become one of believing that we deserve the bad, almost anyone else seems more deserving of good than we do.

Our self-concept has been shaped in part by life circumstances we may deeply regret. Some of us have more pain; some of us have less. This doesn't mean that those of us with less pain have no right or reason to change. It does mean that we can each set our own unique agenda for change.

As we begin to explore options for change — the focus of much of the rest of this book — I urge you to look only at your own pain and consider ways to enhance your own healing. Remind yourself that there is already much to value and love about yourself.

As your self-concept changes — as you come to see yourself as more lovable, worthy, and self-directing — you may find yourself straining to "make yourself right" right now. Go slow. There are endless possibilities for coming even closer to your core-self knowing of right, truth, and virtue. It will take time to choose the ones that fit for you.

PART II:

THE SHAME-
ANXIETY CYCLE

CHAPTER FIVE

THE SHAME-ANXIETY CYCLE

Introduction to the Shame-Anxiety Cycle

We humans seem to have a natural bent for creating order. We name things, count things, invent categories, and look for reasons to explain why things happen in our lives.

So it goes with the experience of shame. We come up with reasons for it: "I don't deserve the good," or "I deserve the bad."

We try to reduce our shame response to a cause-and-effect formula: "If I do or don't do that . . . then I won't feel . . . ." We try to wish shame away with thoughts like, "If I don't drink again . . . ," "If I just avoid my dad . . . ," "If I work really hard at . . . ," " . . . then I won't feel these horrible, rotten feelings."

The *shame-anxiety cycle*, illustrated on page 38, is a model that helps to explain the interrelationships between shame, how we feel it, how we show it, and what we think about it. It has proven useful to people who are severely disabled by shame, as well as to those who are affected but not crippled. It can serve as a guide for using shame as a change-agent for living more fully, lovingly, and joyfully.

The shame-anxiety cycle breaks down the experience of shame into individual phases that are easier to understand and address than shame as a whole. As we study the cycle, we will learn that each phase reacts to and is dependent on the others. We will see that our cause-and-effect thinking can actually keep us trapped in shame-based ways of feeling, behaving, and thinking.

For purposes of explanation, the phases are numbered, but as with any cycle there is no starting or ending point.

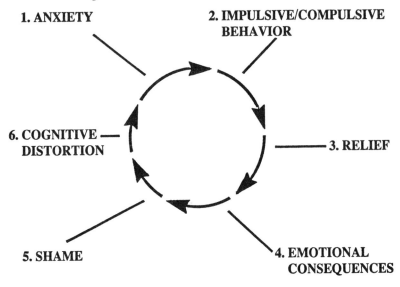

1. ANXIETY
2. IMPULSIVE/COMPULSIVE BEHAVIOR
6. COGNITIVE DISTORTION
3. RELIEF
5. SHAME
4. EMOTIONAL CONSEQUENCES

Before exploring these phases in detail, let's look briefly at each to get an overall picture.

Brief Explanation of the Shame-Anxiety Cycle

During the *anxiety* phase (1), we feel tense, jittery, uptight, queasy, itchy, antsy. We all have our own words to describe this feeling, and we all have our own physical signs that we are experiencing anxiety. Some people feel a tightness across the shoulders. Others shake or tremble, feel dizzy or lightheaded, feel as if there's a knot in their throats or stomachs, or restlessly tap their toes. Still others have a sense of dread that doesn't seem connected to anything specific.

> **Nettie** spoke of her anxiety as, " . . . when I get like that!" "I get like that every time I'm around my mother." "When I get like that, I just can't seem to keep my mind on my work." "Every time I see a movie or something in the newspaper about kids getting hurt, I get like that."
>
> Those words were her verbal shorthand, a term that had come to describe a jittery sensation, racing pulse and heart rate, rapid breathing, a feeling of foreboding. In Nettie's situation, the anxiety had originated in childhood abuse. It had become such a familiar part of her being that she accepted it as "natural." Recognizing "when I get like that" for what it really was — anxiety — was a crucial step toward breaking the shame-anxiety cycle.

Generally, anxiety grows from a low level to a more intense level, although it may seem to hit suddenly without warning. It builds until it can be the driving force behind *impulsive/compulsive behavior* (2).

Many of us get hooked into thinking that if we could just stop a particular behavior we're ashamed of, or get someone else to stop a particular behavior that's painful or shameful to us, our lives would change and everything would be all right. If we could just quit yelling at the kids . . . drinking/using other drugs . . . spending money we don't want to spend for things we don't want or need . . . binge eating sweets . . . engaging in meaningless sex . . . being hurt by someone we love . . . . But it doesn't work. Even when the behavior is stopped or interrupted for a while, we discover that real change isn't that simple.

> When **Nettie** would "get like that"—become highly anxious—she would grab the telephone to call her older sister, Nancy, who lived in another state. As they talked, Nettie would begin to relax until she felt calm enough to hang up. At times the conversation might last an hour or two. During periods of extended anxiety she might find herself calling Nancy daily.
>
> Nettie would "try to fight it," resisting the compulsion to call until she would "just lose control." Thus she frequently called her sister late at night. Sometimes she would "fight it" through a sleepless night, then call early in the morning.
>
> Nettie's phone bills were astronomical. She was frequently at risk of losing phone service because she couldn't pay the charges when they came due. She would become even more anxious at the possibility of "losing her lifeline" to her sister.

After the impulsive/compulsive behavior has occurred, we usually feel a brief period of *relief* (3). The anxiety is gone! Sometimes this is called a "honeymoon period" because it feels so good and it usually doesn't last very long. It is followed closely and quickly by *emotional consequences* (4).

> For **Nettie,** the ending of the period of relief would coincide with hanging up the telephone. She would cringe as she looked at the clock. Feeling guilty about the call, she immediately anticipated financial stress. "I hate myself," she would say. "I swore I wouldn't call Nancy this week. There's the bill — it's getting out of hand again. And Nancy's beginning to get really impatient with me. I'm afraid if I keep bugging her she'll get mad and won't even talk to me. Then what'll I do?"

The emotional consequences of our impulsive/compulsive behavior are almost always uncomfortable. We really don't feel very good about what we've done or what's been done to us. We may feel disappointed, confused, inadequate, dejected, helpless, fearful, angry, guilty, or a combination of these feelings, which usually come flooding in with great intensity and strength. And right behind them is *shame* (5).

Not only did **Nettie** feel shame about her behavior — her compulsive calls to her sister — she felt shame about her need for comfort. She compared herself to her younger sister, Therese, and found herself "not as strong" as she, who "manages just fine by herself." She refused to call other people from the support group she had begun to attend because "I'd die if they knew how crazy I feel." She felt exposed and vulnerable, somehow defective, believing herself "less than" those around her.

Having behaved in a way we don't feel very good about leaves us feeling exposed to ourselves and others as bad, worthless, unlovable. We feel exceedingly vulnerable and unprotected. This feeling is so uncomfortable that we don't want to dwell on it, so we hurry into *cognitive distortion* (6).

People in 12-Step programs (Alcoholics Anonymous, Al-Anon, Overeaters Anonymous, Parents Anonymous, and so on) have another name for cognitive distortion. They call it "stinking thinking." Stinking thinking is filled with words like, "I've got to . . . ," "I have to . . . ," "You never . . . ," "I always . . . ," "I must . . . ," "We should . . . " — demanding, commanding, pressuring, anxiety-provoking words. They symbolize patterns of warped perceptions and irrational thoughts.

"I shouldn't have to call Nancy," **Nettie** would assert. "It was one thing to run to her house for comfort when I was little, but I should be able to handle things by myself now. After all, I'm twenty-two years old! I've got to learn how to take care of myself." As Nettie worked in therapy, she began to see how she pressured herself and others with rigid beliefs about how life "should be."

She also saw the stinking thinking when she justified her compulsive phone calls with, "But you know it's a lot better to call Nancy than go down to the bar to relax. I was beginning to be afraid I'm an alcoholic so I wouldn't want to go out drinking when I get like that."

Cognitive distortion leads us back to anxiety, which is followed by impulsive/compulsive behavior, and the cycle repeats itself again and again. We begin to feel as if we're trapped on a merry-go-round.

It is important to note that whenever we enter the shame-anxiety cycle, all of the phases are set in motion, whirling so quickly that it is very difficult to determine what is really happening. One of my treatment groups called this cycle a "flywheel" because it moves so fast and has so much power.

It is also important to understand that the cycle is not nearly so neat and orderly as the illustration. The phases may blur together. Our anxiety may be so consuming that we are not aware of the other phases — impulsive/

compulsive behavior, relief, emotional consequences, shame, cognitive distortion. We may move back and forth between phases rather than completing the cycle.

Like most of life, there are few things that can be tidily compartmentalized, and shame isn't one of them. But the shame-anxiety cycle can give us a way to approach the experience, and it can give us a framework for change.

Denial and Minimization

A critical factor in staying trapped in the shame-anxiety cycle is our inability to recognize what's happening to us. Because shame-based living and feeling are so emotionally uncomfortable, we train ourselves to repress the emotional trauma we feel. We push it down, out of our conscious awareness; we "stuff it" so we don't have to deal with it.

Denial (the refusal to acknowledge a powerful reality) and *minimization* (the tendency to diminish or downplay a painful reality) are two ways we avoid facing our pain. They fuel the shame-anxiety cycle at every phase.

To draw a homely analogy, imagine a plastic garbage bag. Now imagine slinging it over your shoulder and carrying it with you everywhere. Whenever you encounter an unpleasant or shaming situation, you toss the emotional consequences (guilt, anger, disappointment, and so on) into your garbage bag.

The bag gets heavier and heavier. You start to feel emotionally drained and exhausted from carrying it around. Of course, you throw these feelings into the bag, too! Gradually it fills to capacity.

Then one day you toss one more emotion into your overloaded garbage bag, and suddenly it bursts, spewing its contents on you and others and littering the scenery. In great emotional distress, you probably perform some impulsive/compulsive behavior — bursting into anger, eating, shopping, drinking, whatever.

A frightening aspect of the garbage bag bursting is that the size and ferocity of the explosion seem unconnected to the importance of the final bit of emotional trash tossed into the bag. People often say, "I don't even remember what we were fighting about," or, "It just doesn't seem like what happened was such a big deal." Of course there are times when the shaming situation or incident is very significant, but usually the bag bursts because it simply can't hold any more stuffing, minimization, and denial.

Let's add to this analogy a simple biology lesson. The garbage you have deposited in your bag — the emotional equivalent of orange peels, coffee grounds, moldy fruits and sour milk — is subject to anaerobic decomposition. Deprived of sunlight and oxygen (which speeds quicker, cleaner decomposition), it is dark and warm from being carried close to your body. The contents within disintegrate into a slimy, smelly, fetid, and exceedingly unpleasant mess (as anyone knows who has ever had a real-life garbage bag burst).

Aerobic decomposition, on the other hand, takes place when you spread out your orange peels and coffee grounds in the open air and sunshine. They dry quickly and are soon converted into nutrients that return to the earth and nourish it.

When we repress or stuff our feelings into the dark of unawareness, they fester and become fetid until they burst out with disastrous results. But when we face our shame and anxiety — when we bring them out into the sun and the air — they can become nutrients for positive change and personal growth.

> **Becky's** mother had brought her to therapy because she was having "screaming fits" — outbursts of rage and anger. After several sessions, Becky reported that she was feeling much better about herself. Her outbursts were less intense and occurred less frequently. When I asked her what she thought had made this improvement possible, she grinned and said in her soft Texas accent, "Well, I'm just not putting so much into my Hefty."

Becky was facing her emotional pain and healing herself. She had interrupted the merry-go-round of her shame-anxiety cycle. You can, too.

Interrupting
the Shame-Anxiety Cycle

The shame-anxiety cycle can help us to understand the pattern of our own responses to shame. It can show us how to start using shame and anxiety as forces for positive change.

Imagine grabbing hold of the "tail" of one of the little arrows in the illustration on page 38. Doing this will alter the balance of the cycle. And just as a merry-go-round will stop if one of its sections gets out of balance, the shame-anxiety cycle will stop if you introduce change into any phase.

The chapters that follow suggest and explain ways you can introduce change into your shame-anxiety cycle.

CHAPTER SIX
ANXIETY

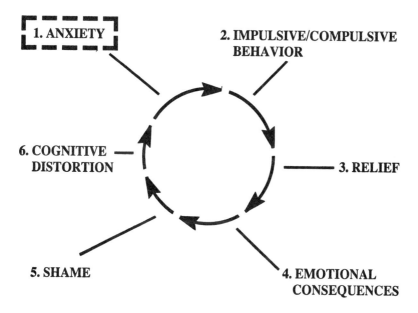

1. ANXIETY

2. IMPULSIVE/COMPULSIVE BEHAVIOR

6. COGNITIVE DISTORTION

3. RELIEF

5. SHAME

4. EMOTIONAL CONSEQUENCES

Understanding Anxiety

People often use the word "anxious" as a synonym for "eager" — as in "I'm anxious to see that new movie," or "I'm anxious to start my vacation." The two are not the same. To feel eager is to anticipate that something good will happen. To feel anxious is to be fearful that something bad is happening or will happen.

When we are anxious, our bodies and minds respond in much the same way as if we were walking through the woods, expecting to come upon a poisonous snake. Even if we never see a snake, our anxiety makes it difficult to enjoy the walk.

43

Like all emotions, anxiety is neither "good" nor "bad." It simply is. For most of us, anxiety is a built-in warning system, a physical and emotional response to our awareness of danger. If we do come across a poisonous snake, anxiety signals us to take precautions. As such, anxiety can be valuable and helpful. It becomes a problem only when we stay anxious for long periods of time, or when our anxiety is not connected to the reality of the situation.

Sources of Anxiety

For some people, anxiety has a biochemical basis. Something has gone awry with their physical functioning, causing ongoing anxious feelings. For those cases, medication can successfully treat anxiety.

For other people, anxiety is a response to an unsafe physical or social environment. Consider the woman who has been living for years with an abusive spouse. She suffers from chronic headaches and stomach pains and takes medication for these complaints. But her real problem is the violent environment — the source of her anxiety and its physical symptoms.

For still other people, anxiety which was a predictable response to a situation in the past has become a habitual response that carries over to the present. Or perhaps we learned from someone important to us to view the world with mistrust. For us, anxiety has become a habitual response to any of the difficulties of daily living, large or small, real or imagined.

Some clues that can help us become aware of habitual anxiety are:

- *Rumination.* This describes a tendency to turn the same thoughts over and over in our minds. If we are still brooding over some slight (real or imagined) that occurred some period of time ago, we are probably ruminating — a sign that we are "holding on" to the past.

- *Worrying.* Just as a dog "worries" a bone, chewing on it, shaking it back and forth, putting it aside only to take it up to chew on again, we may find ourselves coming back to the "same old worry," expending our energies with no resulting sense of satisfaction.

- *Blaming ourselves or others.* Basically, blaming is a way we try to focus our anxiety, as though we can get rid of it if we can find a hook to hang it on. Instead, it keeps hanging around and doesn't go away. It becomes habitual.

- *Asking why.* It's as though we refuse to go on with our lives until we can answer "why" things were the way they were. Predictably, we are stymied because there often are no answers to "why" — which keeps us stuck in the past.

Whatever its source, anxiety can make us so uncomfortable that we will do almost anything to find relief.

When **Sally** forgot the punchline of her story and stomped away from the campfire, her anger began to cool. She felt ashamed. She judged her behavior as "childish." She couldn't imagine going back to face the others, even though she had enjoyed being part of the group before the storytelling incident. The next morning, she was careful to sit apart from the group during the worship service, and she avoided eye contact with anyone who had been at the campfire.

Sally's anxiety at being exposed as a "lousy storyteller" stayed with her for several days. It returned whenever she thought about going to church and seeing the others from the group. The more anxious she felt, the more ashamed she became, and the more she withdrew from the others, which made her feel even more anxious and ashamed . . . and on and on. She was caught in the shame-anxiety cycle.

Responses to Anxiety

When we are in the shame-anxiety cycle, we learn to repress our shame and stuff it. We learn always to be on guard against feeling our shame and letting others see it. We believe that we can't risk exposing our inner self, which we have come to see as helpless and unlovable. We fear being rejected, treated with contempt, or abandoned.

We can also learn to repress and stuff our anxiety. Usually an unconscious choice, this seems preferable to dealing with these intensely uncomfortable feelings.

"What should I do when my daughter won't eat her dinner?" **Susan** implored with tears in her eyes. The evening before, she had sent her daughter away from the table without dessert because she had refused to eat the main dish Susan had prepared. Her anxiety seemed out of proportion to the relatively minor incident she was describing. When I suggested that she might be overreacting, she immediately became defensive. "I can't be wrong!" she exclaimed, her eyes widening. To her, there was no room for error in childrearing.

As we talked further, Susan was able to tie this irrational belief to a longstanding fear that she would be abandoned if she were wrong. When she was a child, her parents had often threatened her. On family car trips, for example, they would say, "Quit that giggling or we're pulling over here and you can just get out!" Years later, in her abusive marriage, her husband had also threatened her: "Serve me another meal like that and it's all over!" No wonder Susan grew anxious at the thought of being wrong or making the slightest error!

I'm reminded of a game often found at amusement centers. There's a big box with many holes in the top, out of which funny little heads pop up unexpectedly. The object of the game is to bop the heads with a rubber mallet whenever they appear. As you successfully bop one after another, the pace quickens until the heads are popping up so quickly that only the most coordinated player can bop them all.

Our unconscious mind seems to recognize uncomfortable feelings that pop to the surface of our conscious mind — and bops them on the head to push them back down again. But just as one tires of playing amusement center games, our minds and bodies tire of repressing these feelings. Our risk of exposure increases and our anxiety grows.

Chaos and Rigidity as Triggers for Anxiety

From the time we are born, we humans need order — predictability, reliability, harmony, and respect for one another's boundaries — if we are to thrive emotionally and physically. Chaos makes it impossible to meet this need.

"I would be so afraid," **Amanda** said. "It was like Mom and Dad were competing to see who would get mad first so they could go slamming off to the bar for the night. Then I'd be stuck with my big sister, who would beat me up at the slightest excuse — then beat me even worse if I told Mom or Dad! Now that I'm older I can see they expected way too much from her. It's no wonder she was frustrated and resentful of me. But as a kid I never knew when the least thing would set one of them off — and I'd end up in tears because I hurt so bad. Now, just let someone look at me sideways, and I start shaking."

Rigidity — too much order — can be just as harmful as chaos. In a rigid, inflexible environment, the individual must deny his or her own needs and submit to the needs and expectations of others.

"My life was just the opposite," **Bob** told me. "You could set your clocks by my parents. Rules were rules. We knew exactly what was expected — but we were afraid that we couldn't do it well enough to satisfy our father. He was really rough on us. No violence, but I remember once he didn't speak to my brother for three weeks because my brother broke a hammer handle when he was building a fort down by the river. He said my brother had to learn respect for other people's property. I would get so scared because my brother was kind of a rebel, and I could see he was headed for trouble every time."

The need for security can be expressed as a desire for what Leon Wurmser calls "love at its peak . . . being as fully accepted as is humanly possible." This is love without threat of abandonment, without violation of our boundaries, without being treated as an object, without being victimized by violence.

In the absence of predictability, reliability, harmony, and respect for our boundaries, we feel out of control and exposed, anxious and ashamed. We respond with hypervigilance or by shutting down.

Hypervigilance

Recall that our core self is surrounded by boundaries with access points that open and close. Our access points allow us to send and receive information to and from our environment, and to make contact with others.

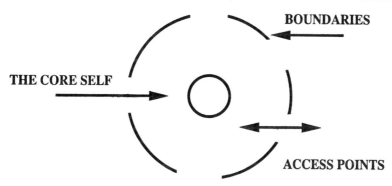

Here is how chaos and rigidity can affect our core self and boundaries:

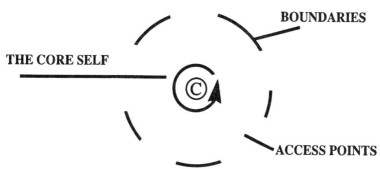

- Our *core self* becomes hypervigilant, scoping out the environment like a radar. We look for danger signs or read cues from others to determine how we can think and act most safely. We are aware of subtleties that other people miss — a tensed muscle in the jaw, a sexual tension, a threatening air about a person.

- Our *boundaries* lose definition, making it harder to distinguish our self from others. (For example: Someone criticizes your parents, and you feel shame.)
- Our *access points* open wider because of our need to be alert to the presence of risk in our environment.

We have little or no control over a chaotic or rigid world. A battered wife can seldom muster the physical strength to stop her more powerful husband from hurting her. Children can't prevent their parents from imposing rules and regulations that are impossible to adhere to.

In an attempt to protect ourselves from the effects of chaos or rigidity, we monitor our environment and let more information in. And this makes us even more anxious! Our core self is assaulted with information, resulting in information overload. And because we have less control over the kind and quantity of information we let out, we risk exposing ourselves. Meanwhile our core self becomes exhausted with too much monitoring.

> **Marea** describes her years of lying awake in the dark, terrified that "tonight would be the night" that more abuse would occur at her father's hands. As she talks, I can almost picture the tiny child she was, clutching her stuffed elephant and baby doll to her chest, wide-eyed in fear. She is unable to see whether danger is approaching. She is watching, watching, looking first at one part of the room and then another. Her eyes strain in the dark, struggling in the only way she can to gain some control over her chaotic environment.

I believe that Marea's habitual anxiety began at that point in her life, as she turned like a radar to detect her abusive father's approach. In a situation where one is truly powerless, hypervigilance is essential to survival. The emotional costs of hypervigilance are heightened anxiety and shame.

Shutting Down

As an alternative to hypervigilance, we may shut down our access points and withdraw from the world. The emotional costs are equally high.

My clients have used many terms to describe this process: "blocking," "numbing out," "tuning out," "going black," "detaching," "unhooking." What is really taking place is a sort of self-hypnosis that provides some relief from anxiety. This may be an entirely unconscious act, or it may be conscious and deliberate.

> "Whenever Dad would launch into one of his tirades," **Arlo** explained, "I'd just go up to my bedroom and zone out — watch TV, listen to the stereo, maybe read a book. It got so he could get roaring drunk and I'd never hear a thing! It's really

causing me problems now. If my kids get a little noisy, I just 'zone out' and leave my wife to handle it. She's getting really angry with me."

Another client shared a puzzling situation. "I can't understand it," **Lorraine** said. "Sex with my husband has never been really good, but lately when he touches my body, my mind just gets up out of bed and is gone."

Interrupting Anxiety

As we drew to the end of our final therapy session, **Colin** said, "I really can't believe the freedom I feel now. I have more energy. I have hope. I'm enjoying my friendships and my family more each day. Looking back, it's hard to understand why I didn't realize how anxious I felt. I thought that was how people were supposed to feel!"

Like Colin, many of us have difficulty recognizing our anxiety as a problem because it has become "natural" and habitual for us. We don't realize there is any other way to feel! Even when it reaches an acute stage, we may minimize or deny its intensity.

When **Lance** became over-anxious, he would explode verbally with profanity and aggressive language. He didn't understand why those around him grew frightened and alienated during his outbursts. He described his behavior simply as, "I guess I got a little excited."

Recognizing the Signs

We all have our own anxiety signs — indications that our anxiety is rising to an uncomfortable or unhealthy level. These might include:

- *Physical signs:* Headache, sore muscles, trembling, stomach discomfort, itching or hives, nail-biting, tapping fingers or toes, trouble swallowing

- *Emotional signs:* Crying, withdrawal, wanting to run away or hide, suspiciousness, jealousy, a sense of impending doom, extreme mood swings, demanding attention when you don't get what you want

- *Spiritual signs:* Excessive dependence on others or excessive self-reliance, feeling isolated, feeling unlovable, inability to trust others, lack of faith in God, giving up easily on relationships or tasks, being overly judgmental

- *Intellectual signs:* Ruminating (letting your mind dwell on the same thing or incident again and again), racing thoughts, forgetfulness, dwelling on the future, daydreaming, repetitive thoughts, saying the same thing again and again

Unfortunately, we often fail to recognize our anxiety signs, or we choose to ignore them and hope they'll go away. But which is easier — to catch a barrel when it first tips over, or to try to grab it as it's rolling madly down a hill? It's much easier to interrupt low-level anxiety than to wait until it has gathered strength and force. It's much harder to calm ourselves when we feel like we're about to fly off the handle or fall apart.

But "harder" doesn't mean "impossible." The tools and techniques described below can help you to reduce and manage anxiety at almost any stage.

Tools and Techniques for Interrupting Anxiety

Before you try any of these anxiety-interrupters, it's important to caution you that none represents a quick fix or cure. Each takes time, effort, and commitment. As you choose those that seem right for you, consider these tips:

- They will be more effective if you use them when your anxiety level is low.

- They will be more effective if you practice them every day.

The Anxiety Log

I consider the Anxiety Log to be the #1 most useful tool for managing anxiety. It increases your awareness of the low-level anxiety that can pull you into the shame-anxiety cycle. It points out harmful thoughts and behaviors and reveals patterns you can change. And it serves as a written record of your personal progress in freeing yourself from the shame-anxiety cycle.

All you need to keep an Anxiety Log is paper and something to write with. Use the form shown on page 51. Each item on the form is explained on pages 52-54.

Your Anxiety Log will be most effective if you follow these simple guidelines:

- Do at least one entry a day for a minimum of six weeks. In my experience, the first few times people try filling out Anxiety Logs, they come back and report, "I had a great week. I didn't get upset once." Usually what this means is that they didn't feel intensely anxious. Everyone feels some anxiety or tension every day. In fact, most people report feeling some anxiety 8-10 times a day.

- Do your entry immediately after the anxiety episode you want to log (or as soon as possible). You'll want your thoughts and behaviors to be fresh in your mind when you log them.
- Be patient and persistent. In time, you should start being able to detect low-level anxiety before the barrel starts rolling downhill.

ANXIETY LOG

1. Trigger: _____

2. Anxiety level: _____

3. Irrational thoughts: _____

_____

_____

4. How I behaved: _____

_____

5. How I would rate my behavior (plus or minus): _____

_____

6. Rational thoughts: _____

_____

_____

7. How I would behave in the future: _____

_____

_____

_____

_____

1. *Trigger.* This is the external event or situation that existed immediately before your awareness of your anxiety. It wasn't the cause of your anxiety; it was the incident to which you responded with anxiety.

Limit your description to "just the facts." Stick to what happened, not why it happened or who was involved (or at fault). For example: "A glass of milk was spilled," not "Amy was fooling around at the dinner table and spilled her milk again."

At first you may find yourself writing detailed reports. Let them sit for a couple of days, then reread them. Do they sound as if you're justifying your behavior or trying to prove that someone else deserved to be treated the way you acted? Try to isolate one tiny part of each incident as the real trigger. Keep it simple!

2. *Anxiety level.* On a scale of 1 to 10, with 10 being the highest, rate the level of anxiety you were feeling when you first became aware of your anxiety. This rating is personal to you only — an indication of how you felt, not how someone else thought you felt or how you felt in comparison to someone else. It should not be a judgment of how you behaved; we'll look at behavior in a moment.

If you get stuck, try this approach: Assign one (1) point to each anxiety sign you feel — tension in your shoulders, butterflies in your stomach, crying, forgetfulness, and so on. Then add up the points to determine your anxiety score.

3. *Irrational thoughts.* You probably had irrational thoughts without being conscious of them. These are the thoughts that flash immediately into your mind in response to the trigger. At this point you probably won't be aware that they increase your anxiety. How you think is a habit. It feels "natural."

Try to catch those first words that you say to yourself and others. You may have had blaming thoughts about yourself or others. For example, "If only Amy would be more careful with her milk, I wouldn't be so nervous during dinner."

Irrational thoughts are usually followed by more irrational thoughts — "got to," "have to," "never," "always," "must," "should." For example: "Amy should know better. She's got to learn to keep her elbows off the table."

Log all of the irrational thoughts you can recall that relate to the anxiety incident. Don't elaborate on them or edit them; just write them down.

4. *How I behaved.* Your behavior is what you actually did, not how you felt or thought. This should be a description of how you acted during

the incident you are logging. It may help to ask yourself, "If someone else had been watching me, what would they have seen?"

Again, keep it simple and log just the facts. For example: "I yelled at Amy and sent her to bed," not "I acted like a stupid idiot." Don't blame or judge yourself; negative self-talk only creates more anxiety.

5. *How I would rate my behavior (plus or minus).* This is a bottom-line assessment: Was your behavior appropriate? If your answer is yes, give it a plus; if your answer is no, give it a minus.

It doesn't matter whether you behaved the way you wanted to, or whether you wish you had behaved differently. Nor is this a measure of whether you got the results you wanted. Just write a plus or a minus.

6. *Rational thoughts.* Your anxiety level probably decreased at some point after the incident. By identifying the rational, calming thoughts that worked for you at this stage of the shame-anxiety cycle, you can begin to develop a repertoire of such thoughts to use whenever you feel your anxiety rising.

For example: Instead of blaming, yelling, or punishing Amy for spilling her milk, you can think, "No need to get excited. She didn't mean to spill her milk. Even if she did, I can still be responsible for acting in a way I feel good about."

Be aware of one pitfall: the possibility that you are stuffing your feelings about the incident. Rational thinking and stuffing may appear to be similar, but they have very different effects. Rational thoughts help to reduce and manage anxiety; stuffing adds to your bag of emotional garbage.

For example: "Amy spilled her milk; these things happen" can be an anxiety-reducing, rational thought. However, if it's followed by, "What does it matter if I'm tired of cleaning up messes?" or something similar, you're probably stuffing. Any variation on I-don't-deserve-the-good or I-do-deserve-the-bad is a sure sign of stuffing. It reinforces our feelings of helplessness and shame.

If you have difficulty identifying rational thoughts to use in this stage, memorize a slogan or affirmation that can be used in many situations. Some of the 12-Step slogans are useful: "Easy does it." "Keep it simple." "Let go and let God." Affirm your ability to calm yourself: "I can handle this. I can slow down and develop a plan. No need to blame myself or others."

7. *How I would behave in the future.* Would you feel better about yourself if you could change the way you behaved? How would you like to handle this type of situation in the future? You can behave differently.

This isn't always easy. For many people, the way they now behave is the only way they know how to behave. They can't see any alternatives to yelling at Amy and sending her to bed.

One powerful alternative is to simply stop a minute before you act to use some rational thinking. There are few situations that demand instant action. If nothing else, stopping to think a moment will change the rhythm of your usual reaction, which will make the next time different.

Think in terms of opposites. For example, instead of yelling at Amy, speak to her quietly. If you would ordinarily withdraw from the situation, stay there as an observer. Perhaps you are the type who stands there and argues to the bitter end; walk away next time.

Other alternatives exist, but you may need help finding them. Ask someone you trust for ideas. Read a book on parenting. If parenting isn't your problem, there are many excellent self-help books available on a variety of other subjects.

A word of caution here: Many people using anxiety logs for the first time will plan alternative behaviors with a particular result in mind. For example: "If I do this certain thing, then Amy won't spill her milk." The purpose of this part of the log is not to think up ways to manage the behavior of others, but to plan more effective ways for you to behave when you are anxious.

As you find more satisfying ways to deal with your anxiety and the related impulsive-compulsive behaviors, you will discover many problems virtually solving themselves — because you are no longer contributing to them with anxiety and irrational thinking.

Diet and Nutrition

When we believe that we don't deserve the good, a possible consequence may be to neglect the proper care of our bodies — to behave as if they don't deserve to be well fed, exercised, and refreshed with enough sleep.

Many people maintain their cars better than they do their bodies. Few of us would deliberately put the wrong kind of gas in our car's fuel tank, yet we fuel our bodies with coffee, chocolate, and caffeinated soft drinks. Caffeine abuse can lead to physical tremors, irritation, the inability to concentrate, rapid pulse rate, and other symptoms that are virtually identical to anxiety symptoms. In fact, the mind interprets them as anxiety symptoms and responds with thoughts like, "Something is going on here that I don't feel good about. Something must be wrong. I need to be on guard." These thoughts lead to more anxiety, and suddenly we trip back into the shame-anxiety cycle.

The nicotine in cigarettes, and the refined sugar in sweets, can also create anxiety-like symptoms in the body. Some chemical additives and dyes in processed foods have been linked to hyperactivity in children and may have other side-effects. Many popular weight-loss diets promote inadequate or imbalanced nutritional intake which may result in fatigue, trembling, light-headedness, hot or cold flashes, irritability, hypervigilance — all anxiety-like symptoms.

Are you taking good care of your body? The next time you sit down to eat, ask yourself, "Would I serve this to my best friend?" If your answer is no, it's time to consider how and why you're denying your own physical needs. Learn more about diet and nutrition and change your habits accordingly. Some of your anxiety may lessen or disappear as you start making better, healthier choices.

Physical Exercise

Physical exercise is an excellent way to relieve anxiety. Many people find some form of aerobic exercise to be most effective. Walking, running, biking, jumping rope, and other activities that increase heart rate and oxygen intake are superb antidotes to the physical consequences of anxiety. Aerobic dance provides the added benefits of music and rhythm, which satisfy emotional and spiritual needs. Yoga and other stretching-and-limbering exercises combine mental concentration with physical exercise to help diminish racing thoughts and ruminations. Team sports can be fun, but beware of placing too much emphasis on competition, or you may actually increase your anxiety level.

Exercise is a lot like eating your vegetables. We think that we "should," but it's easy to stop at good intentions. In fact, our shoulds can set us up for failure. When you sternly tell yourself, "You should get out and walk," there is probably a small voice inside saying, " . . . but I'm not going to."

If you tell yourself, "I'll try to walk four times this week," you are probably hedging in your commitment. Hidden behind the word "try" are your real thoughts: "I'll probably fail," "I'm not really serious about this," or "I don't really want to do this." Instead, think, "I am going to walk four times this week."

If you're not in the exercise habit, choose an easily achievable goal — a baby step in the direction of taking better care of yourself. And make it specific. For example: "I'm going to walk once this week for 15 minutes." A "do-able" goal can give you a sense of achievement that fuels you for the next step.

Mental Exercise

Mental exercises can be useful anxiety-interrupters. Many people complain that they can't turn off their thoughts when they go to bed at night. They have trouble concentrating; they go over and over the same worries; they experience racing or tumultuous thoughts. Simple relaxation exercises can help to alleviate these anxiety symptoms. Here is one you can try:

Step 1: Making yourself comfortable, close your eyes.

Step 2: Say out loud, fairly emphatically, "STOP."

Step 3: Substitute a calming mental image, such as a picture of your favorite outdoor spot.

If necessary, repeat steps 2 and 3.

Step 4: Pull the picture into your mind for a slow count of five. Gradually increase the count until you can hold the scene in your mind for a count of sixty.

Step 5: Let go of the image at the end of the count and turn your attention to something different than the event or situation that originally triggered your anxiety.

If necessary, repeat from step 1.

Learning a new way to interrupt anxiety buildup will be more effective if you try it when your anxiety level is low. Daily practice will build confidence in your new skill.

Advance Planning

The time to plan how to deal with anxiety is not when you are in the midst of an anxiety attack. Like a vacuum filled with air, there's no room for rational thought once anxious thoughts have rushed into the mind.

Instead, pick a time when you are feeling less anxious than usual and list some positive ways you have found to reduce your anxiety. Start your list with at least three techniques that don't require major effort (like driving to the fitness clinic and working out on exercise machines — save those for later!). The next time you become aware that your anxiety is rising, go to your list, choose one idea, and do it.

Some ideas for your list might include:

• Do the STOP imagery exercise from page 56.

• Read the meditation for the day from your church, or read a 12-Step program meditation booklet.

• Go outdoors and walk around the block — or even around your house or apartment building.

• Take a warm bath.

• Log what you are feeling and thinking at this moment.

Don't "try" it; do it! Even if you don't succeed in reducing your anxiety, you'll experience the satisfaction of making a positive effort on your own behalf. It will get easier, and soon you'll establish a pattern you can count on.

Alcohol/Other Drugs and Dependence

Many people, when they start feeling anxious, reach for a drink or a pill to help them calm down or relax. But the use of alcohol/other drugs can be a form of self-medication, of stuffing uncomfortable feelings. And the use of anything outside ourselves to deal with a condition inside ourselves can lead to increased dependence and even addiction.

When we become dependent, we deny our own power to act. We reinforce our shame-based belief that we don't deserve the good — that we don't deserve to be self-directing, self-regulating, self-nurturing. We reinforce our belief that we deserve the bad — to feel anxious, helpless, and full of shame.

Many anxious individuals have found mutual support and healing in Emotions Anonymous (E.A.), a nationwide organization based on the 12-Step principles of Alcoholics Anonymous (A.A.). Attending an E.A. or other 12-Step group meeting can help you understand the difference between dependence and the power of caring. Twelve-Step groups are practical examples of how admitting, facing, and accepting a problem can bring about positive change.

To find an E.A. group or other 12-Step groups in your area, check your local telephone directory. Or see the Resources section on pages 149-150 of this book.

CHAPTER SEVEN

IMPULSIVE/COMPULSIVE BEHAVIOR

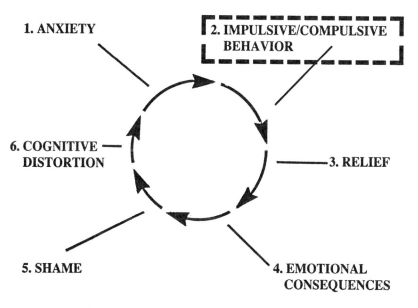

Behavior as a Response to Anxiety

When you ask most people what they would like to change about themselves, they usually name a specific behavior: "I'd like to quit smoking," "I need to go on a diet," "I wish I would exercise more," "I want to be able to walk past a bargain without pulling out my charge card." They would like to change something they do.

When anxiety builds inside us and we become increasingly uncomfortable — stressed out, shaking, faint, heart-pounding, can't-breathe — we often feel the urge to do something about it. And since we are creatures of habit, we fall back on habitual behaviors. We tap our toes, step outside for a breath of fresh air, get irritable and snappish.

In most cases, our anxiety-related behavior is relatively harmless. It doesn't upset our lives or our relationships. We don't enjoy being uncomfortable, but we recognize that it's part of being human, and we know that it will pass.

In other cases, though, the anxiety level rises so high and the internal pressure becomes so strong that we believe we just can't stand it anymore. We feel compelled to do something — anything — to get some relief. So we perform an *impulsive* act — one we commit rashly, hastily, without due consideration. Or we fall back on a *compulsive* act — a repeated, habitual behavior we feel compelled to perform to gain relief. Because we are acting under pressure, we feel out of control and ashamed. We try to hide our impulsive/compulsive behavior from others. And this makes us even more ashamed.

On the surface, eating a dish of chocolate ice cream doesn't seem connected to the shame-anxiety cycle. But this behavior takes on a different complexion if one is a compulsive over-eater. We may feel ashamed about eating ice cream to relieve our anxiety because we believe we're "giving in" to our behavior. The shame triggers more anxiety; we eat more ice cream. We hide the empty cartons at the bottom of the trash. And on and on it goes.

We get hooked into thinking that if only we could stop our impulsive/compulsive behavior, everything would be fine. We would feel all right if only we could stop yelling at the kids, taking a drink, binge-eating sweets, getting high, engaging in meaningless sex, buying yet another gadget we don't need and won't use. . . . But even if we do stop, we don't feel better. We are still plagued with anxiety and worried about our ability to remain abstinent from the problem behavior.

Our thinking fuels both our anxiety and our impulsive/compulsive behavior. Here's how it goes:

I do "it" (the behavior) .... I feel bad/anxious.

I feel bad/anxious .... I think I'll feel better if I quit doing "it."

I quit doing "it" .... but I still feel bad/anxious.

I feel bad/anxious .... so I might as well do "it."

I do "it" .... I feel bad/anxious.

Some researchers in the area of compulsive behavior call this the "what-the-hell" syndrome. If the situation can't be fixed right now and just right, then what-the-hell, we might as well quit trying!

Paradoxically, the harder we try to control the problem behavior, the more out-of-control we feel. We think about the problem behavior all or most of the time. The more we think about not thinking about it, the heavier it weighs on our minds — and the more likely we are to do it! We end up giving the problem behavior top priority in our lives.

Tools and Techniques for Interrupting Impulsive/Compulsive Behavior

Just as we can learn to interrupt anxiety, we can learn to interrupt the impulsive/compulsive behavior that is our response to anxiety. Following are some tools and techniques for you to try. Remember that these will work best when your anxiety level is low, and if you practice them often.

Take a Time-Out

A time-out is a wonderfully effective way to interrupt your own impulsive/compulsive behavior. Here's how it works:

1. When you first recognize that your anxiety is building, announce to yourself and/or others, "I'm starting to feel anxious. I'm going to take a time-out. I'll be back shortly." By saying these words, you take ownership of your anxiety. You bring it out in the open instead of hiding it or stuffing it.

2. Now remove yourself from the immediate environment. Go for a walk or a brief run. (If you're at work, you might duck into the restroom.) Don't go for a drive or a bike ride; the purpose of your time-out is to allow you to focus on anxiety reduction without distraction.

3. Spend your time-out on positive self-talk and relaxation exercises. Quote from *The Little Engine That Could:* "I think I can . . . I think I can . . . I think I can." No have tos, shoulds, musts, or gottas allowed! Concentrate on what you can do: "I may not feel comfortable, but I can face my anxiety . . . There are some situations I can't control, but I can control my behavior for this moment . . . I can handle myself in a way I feel good about by taking a break and allowing myself to grow calm again."

Deep breathing is a relaxation exercise you can do anytime,

anyplace. Inhale as deeply as possible . . . hold your breath for a slow count of five . . . exhale as completely as possible. Repeat until you start to feel the anxiety draining from your body. Enhance the effectiveness of this exercise by closing your eyes and imagining the fresh, clean air moving into your lungs, absorbing your tension, and removing your tension as it leaves your body.

4. Return from your time-out when you feel ready — when the urge to perform the impulsive/compulsive behavior has lessened or gone away, when your mind is calm and clear. Going back to the situation you left is important not only as an affirmation of your ability to care for yourself; it's also a signal to others that you intend to be responsible for yourself.

Accentuate the Positive

In the words of the song made famous by Bing Crosby, "You've got to accentuate the positive, eliminate the negative." We are often aware of our desire to "eliminate the negative" behavior. We seldom think of "accentuating the positive" — adding satisfying or self-fulfilling behaviors to our lives. Can you think of a positive that you might want to accentuate?

For some of us, adding regular attendance at church or synagogue might help get our lives back into balance. For others, a positive addition might be to get re-involved in a hobby or activity that has fallen by the wayside. For still others, it might be to substitute a positive behavior for one they see as negative.

Susie's eyes lit up as she exclaimed, "Why, I could go for a walk instead of grabbing a handful of cookies!" She began to see the can dos in her life — the manageable alternatives to her impulsive/compulsive behaviors.

Start Small

It's okay to start small. Even tiny steps in the right direction will eventually get you where you want to go. This is a turnaround in thinking for most of us, who have a tendency to set goals for big, dramatic change. Wanting to make our behavior right — right now! — we pressure ourselves with unrealistic expectations of how much and how fast we can change.

Start by asking yourself, "What's the least amount of change I will settle for?" For example: Rather than decide "I'm never going to use my charge card again," try, "I will leave my charge card at home this week." Or, if that seems too difficult and anxiety-provoking, amend it to "one day this week." And if that causes problems, back off to "I'm going to leave my charge card home this afternoon."

You can apply this technique to almost any behavior. Instead of "I will quit smoking today," tell yourself, "I will go an hour today without a cigarette." Instead of "I will stop eating chocolate ice-cream, period," say, "I will allow myself one helping of chocolate ice-cream today."

Decide What You Really Want

An impulsive/compulsive behavior can be a smokescreen, covering up our shame and anxiety. It can prevent us from asking ourselves, "What is it that I really want?"

Compulsive eating is a clear example. As we stand in front of the refrigerator with the door open, or mindlessly stuff food into our mouths, generally it's not really food that we want. For many of us, food represents comfort, a connection that is first made when we are held and fed as infants. Compulsive eating may be an unconscious attempt to recapture that sense of comfort, of being nurtured and taken care of. The trouble is, it doesn't work. We feel ashamed because our eating is out of control. We abuse our bodies with too much food or the wrong kinds of food. We tell ourselves that if we could only find the right thing to eat, we'd feel better.

What is it that you really want? Ask yourself that question. You may not be able to answer it at first; shame is so closely tied to secrecy that the answer may be buried deep inside you. If you're in the habit of denying or minimizing your needs, you may believe that there's nothing you want. You may not have the words to express what you want.

Keep asking anyway. Log your answers, even if they seem irrelevant or silly. Over time, a pattern should start to emerge.

Following her first week of keeping an anxiety log, **Rachael** read her list aloud: "I want Elliot to come home on time tonight. I want the girls to be quiet so I can rest. I want Beth to go to the movie with me Saturday night."

"It sounds as though I want other people to make me happy!" she realized. The next week she found different answers within herself: "I want to get rid of this jittery feeling inside. I want to be more peaceful. I want to feel connected to my husband and kids." She had begun to recognize what she really wanted to change in her life.

Call a Friend

Pick up the phone and call someone you know and trust, who knows you and understands what you're going through as you struggle with your impulsive/compulsive behavior. Talk about it.

A word of caution: Talking can degenerate into complaining, a compulsive behavior in itself. Complaining increases anxiety because it is by nature negative and blaming. Blaming is a form of irrational thinking, which also increases anxiety.

When you feel the need to talk, choose someone who's been there — someone who's struggled with impulsive/compulsive behavior and has taken positive steps toward change. A 12-Step group is an excellent place to find people you can talk to. There are literally hundreds of different types of 12-Step groups, each organized around the desire to change a problem behavior: overeating, drinking, child abuse, overspending, gambling, and so on. To find out which groups have chapters in your area, check your local telephone directory or contact the Self-Help Clearinghouse; see page 150 of this book.

Keep Track

When we are caught up in the shame-anxiety cycle, it becomes very difficult to be objective about ourselves or our impulsive/compulsive behaviors. Shame-based perceptions can magnify a behavior out of proportion. When that happens, we start judging ourselves by that one small part of ourselves. For example: "I get mad at the kids too often, so I must be a lousy parent." Or: "I don't hang up my clothes until my husband yells at me, so I must be a slob."

Think of a behavior you feel ashamed of — an impulsive/compulsive behavior you wish you could stop. Now count the number of times you actually do it — yell at the kids, grab a handful of cookies, reach for another cigarette.

This may seem like accentuating the negative. Rather, it's a way of focusing on reality. In our shame-based perceptions, we are likely to either exaggerate or minimize and deny the true extent of the problem. Keeping track of our behavior gives us a realistic goal for change. It also helps us know when we succeed in our efforts to change.

Becky was brought to therapy because of her "screaming fits." Her mother claimed that whenever she asked for help around the house, Becky threw a tantrum. I asked the two of them to spend the next week counting Becky's outbursts. They were both surprised to learn that Becky was acting out her anger an average of just twice a day. At other times, she willingly cooperated with her mother's requests for help. Becky felt relieved and far less ashamed of her behavior; her mother was pleased to realize that the problem wasn't as severe as she had perceived it to be. When Becky returned the following week to report only two "screaming fits" all week, she and her mother glowed with satisfaction.

Creative Outlets for Anxiety

Expressing our feelings through a creative medium can be a powerful tool for healing. The same energy that drives our impulsive/compulsive behaviors can be redirected to express ourselves in a more positive fashion.

Let yourself move away from the belief that your creation must be judged. The purpose here is to express yourself in a different way, not to create a piece of art. Listed below are a few suggestions. As you begin to experiment, you will see more possibilities.

- Using clay or children's flour dough, create a sculpture to express your feelings. Try painting or drawing to create a visual image of what is happening to you emotionally. One of my clients creates unique and beautiful paper sculptures to represent feelings and memories that she can't find words to express. Working with your hands can connect you to the here and now, providing genuine relief from anxiety.

- Express your thoughts as poetry. There are many ways to create a poem. (It doesn't have to rhyme.) The equipment is simple and readily available. You can leave your thoughts and emotions on the paper. If you're not ready to write, read aloud poetry that fits your mood.

- Music can be a wonderful way to channel the impulsive/compulsive pressures — especially if you make it yourself. The next time you feel your anxiety building, pick up the guitar, play the piano. If you aren't musically inclined, listen to a favorite recording that reflects your mood. Some people find it helpful to start with intense or dramatic music such as Kachaturian's "Gayne Ballet," then switch to a more relaxing or soothing piece like Handel's "Water Music." Dancing or moving in time to the music can create a sense of harmony between body and soul.

CHAPTER EIGHT
RELIEF

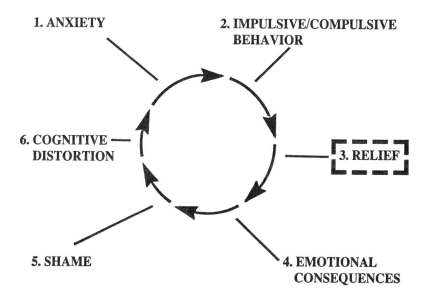

1. ANXIETY

2. IMPULSIVE/COMPULSIVE
   BEHAVIOR

6. COGNITIVE
   DISTORTION

3. RELIEF

5. SHAME

4. EMOTIONAL
   CONSEQUENCES

Interrupting Relief

Why would we want to interrupt the relief phase of the shame-anxiety cycle? On the surface, that doesn't seem logical. Relief from the negative consequences of shame might appear to be our ultimate goal!

In fact, relief as we normally experience it actually works to perpetuate the cycle. When I first began to look at shame issues with clients, I was surprised to hear their answers to questions like, "How did you feel after you hit your wife? . . . went to bed with your neighbor? . . . ate four pizzas? . . . went on that shopping spree?" Very frequently, sometimes in the midst of tears or the emotional agony that had brought them to my office, the answer came resoundingly: "Good!"

As my clients taught me more about the consequences of shame in their lives, I began to realize that what they actually felt was relief — a release from built-up anxiety. "Good" was shorthand for "calmer, less agitated, less fearful of losing control." It seemed to describe an irrational belief that "now things will be okay because I'm never going to do that again!"

To understand how relief contributes to perpetuation of the shame-anxiety cycle, we need to know something about behavior modification.

A Short Course in Behavior Modification

Behavior modification is a psychological method for understanding how and why reinforcement may motivate us to change or continue certain behaviors.

Behaviorists start with the concept of "A-B-C."

- "A" stands for *antecedent* — what comes before a behavior.
- "B" stands for *behavior* — what you do in response to the antecedent.
- "C" stands for *consequence* — what happens as a result of the behavior.

For example:

- "A": You see an advertisement for beer as you are watching television.
- "B": You go to the kitchen to get a beer.
- "C": You drink the beer.

If the consequence (drinking the beer) of your behavior (getting the beer) is acceptable, satisfying, or pleasurable — if the beer tastes good to you, for example — then the next time you see a beer advertisement (the antecedent here), there's a good chance that you will consider repeating the behavior. A consequence that motivates us to repeat a behavior is called a *positive reinforcement.*

A positive reinforcement has nothing to do with the judgment of whether a particular behavior is desirable or not. In this case, we could choose up sides and debate whether drinking beer in response to an ad is a good behavior. If you're on the side of the agency that produced the ad or the company that paid for it, you'd probably argue that yes, it's a good behavior. If you're on the side of people who are concerned about their loved ones' drinking habits, you might well argue that no, it's not.

A consequence that discourages us from repeating a behavior is called a *negative reinforcement.* For example: Christopher wants a cookie. Mother refuses (antecedent). Christopher cries (behavior). If Mother then responds by giving Christopher a cookie (consequence), his behavior has been positively reinforced. The next time Christopher wants a cookie and Mother says no, Christopher will cry until he gets one. But if Mother stands firm in her refusal to hand over the cookie (consequence), Christopher is less likely to cry for cookies in the future because his behavior has been negatively reinforced.

What usually happens in real life — sometimes Christopher gets a cookie, and sometimes he doesn't — is called *intermittent reinforcement.* With intermittent reinforcement, the consequences of a behavior are unpredictable. Yet Christopher keeps crying, even though this behavior works (gets a cookie) only a small percentage of the time.

Intermittent reinforcement is the most powerful way to motivate behavior. It's what keeps us going back to the mailbox even though we've had nothing but junk mail for weeks. It's what keeps the gambler at the slot machine even though she's never won a pot. We persist in believing that "sometime" we'll get a letter, strike it rich, convince Mother to give us a cookie.

Relief as Positive Reinforcement

In the shame-anxiety cycle, relief is the reinforcement, the reason we repeat a behavior no matter how ashamed or anxious we feel following the behavior. If we generally experience relief after the behavior, we have a very powerful reinforcement. For example, if we feel calm, less anxious, or less fearful every time we eat cheesecake, we will probably keep eating cheesecake whenever anxiety builds. This can happen unconsciously, even when we are unaware of the presence of anxiety.

If a behavior is only sometimes (intermittently or unpredictably) followed by relief, this becomes an even more powerful reinforcement. It's as though we're telling ourselves, "I've found it here before. If I just keep looking, I'll find it again."

For those of us who feel trapped in the shame-anxiety cycle, that brief period of relief is comparable to a glass of water to a person lost in the desert. Even though this kind of relief is very short-lived and may have a high cost in terms of our lives and relationships, we become conditioned to use the behavior in our desperate search for a way out of the shame trap.

"As I think about it now," **Sam** said, "I was using running the same way some people use drugs. When three times a week didn't relieve my anxiety, I upped my running until I was out every evening for an hour and a half. My wife Jody hated it. It fouled up our dinner schedule. The kids would get hungry and cranky so she started feeding them a separate meal, and then she started eating with them because she never knew when I'd get back from the gym. By the time I ate, our evening was gone and we had no time to spend together. But I just kept on running, because once or twice a week, sometimes oftener, I would leave the track with the feeling of relief. It generally didn't last long because I'd start feeling so guilty about leaving Jody alone with the kids that I'd often be uptight again by the time I got home to face her."

Genuine vs. Non-Genuine Relief

Relief that follows an impulsive/compulsive behavior is short-lived because it isn't genuine. Genuine relief reinforces positive change and our desire to function at our highest capacity. Non-genuine relief "feels good" while it drags us down.

"Money isn't really the issue here," **Cherie** said. "It's not that we can't afford the things I buy, or that it's putting us in debt. It's that I feel out of control. When I begin to get anxious, I begin to think about going to the mall. I try to fight it, but at some point I feel absolutely compelled to go buy something — anything! It's crazy because lots of times I know while I'm paying for something that I don't want it — but it still feels good. It doesn't last long because I'm so ashamed. I try to hide my packages when I get home, so my husband won't know. I've just got to stop this. I hate myself!"

Consider the compulsive use of alcohol/other drugs. This behavior directly contradicts our *Funktionlust* — our desire to experience our own well-functioning — and interferes with our core-self knowing of good, truth, morality, virtue, rightness. It prevents us from being self-creating and self-directing. We "feel good," but what we are really feeling is relief from painful reality. This reinforces our using behavior while having very negative consequences for ourselves — for example, hangovers, blackouts, withdrawal symptoms, even chemical dependence.

Or consider the family where violence is the norm. It is well-documented that abused family members may actually provoke violent incidents. Waiting for violence to happen is so anxiety-filled that actually being abused is a "relief" from the emotional buildup that precedes an incident.

Denial and Minimization

Denial and minimization are two common ways to find non-genuine relief from the discomfort of the shame-anxiety cycle. They become so routine and habitual that we don't realize when we are using them to stuff our true feelings. If you are denying and minimizing your feelings, the signs listed below may help you become aware of ways you stuff them.

- *Shrugging your shoulders.* This is a valuable body-language clue that we are pushing feelings into our emotional garbage bag. The shrug says, "It's not that big a deal . . . Who cares? So what?"

- *Justifying your own behavior by focusing on the behavior of others.* The key to this form of denial and minimization is the "they"-word. For example: "They just have to learn . . . . " "They should understand . . . . " "By now, they ought to . . . . " Rather than deal with the fact that we're screaming at our kids, we say, "They just have to learn that they need to do their chores right after school." Instead of facing our excessive drinking, we say, "They should understand that I've been under a lot of stress." Or we defend our excessive spending with, "By now, they ought to know that I need decent hunting equipment."

- *Excusing your behavior with "buts."* One of my colleagues maintains that when we use "but" in a sentence, we erase everything that's gone before. For example: "Yes, but . . . . " "I really meant to get here earlier, but . . . . " "Well, maybe I overreacted a little bit, but . . . . " Although we appear to take responsibility for our behavior, it's all just sleight-of-tongue, a way to deny or minimize the consequences of our behavior.

How to Find Genuine Relief

Genuine relief can be described as a feeling of well-being when our sense of pleasure is in harmony with our core-self knowing of good, truth, morality, virtue, rightness. Following are some ways to go about finding genuine relief.

- *Get your shame, anxiety, or impulsive/compulsive behavior out into the open.* This isn't easy to do, since the nature of shame calls for secrecy and hiding.

Let's return for a moment to our garbage-bag analogy. If we spread garbage out under the sun, it begins the natural process of aerobic decomposition — returning to its original elements, nourishing the next generation of plants. But if we stuff garbage into a plastic bag and hide it, anaerobic decomposition takes place. The garbage becomes slimy, stinky, fetid. If we punch a little hole in the bag (if there is an unexpected revelation of our shame), it smells atrocious, we plug our noses, we are repelled.

The relief of getting our secret out into the open is like spreading it out under the sun. It may smell (or hurt) at first, but the fresh air and light quickly begin their healing work.

> **Steve** walked briskly into an expensive restaurant for a lunch meeting with an important new client. As the hostess led Steve to the table, he recognized the client as someone he had known long ago. It was John, who had won the state high-school debate tournament after Steve had blown his own rebuttal! Instantly Steve was swept back in time to the shame he had felt as he failed himself and his teammates. Suddenly he was no longer his company's star account executive. He was a 16-year-old boy, blushing, wanting to dig a hole and jump in. He felt exposed, defective, "less than," helpless to control his nervousness about speaking in public. His stomach tightened and his jaws clenched.

Steve is a successful account executive. Generally, he functions very well in both his business and personal relationships. Here is how he handled this situation:

> **Steve** stopped in his tracks for an instant, immobilized by shame. Recovering quickly, he walked over to John and said, "I didn't recognize your name when we were discussing the account at the office, but seeing you now I remember who you are. You walked away with the trophy the year we debated nuclear disarmament. I was really embarrassed because I blew my rebuttal." John answered, "I don't remember that, but I do remember how scared I was to be at the state tournament in my junior year." The two men started reminiscing about the trials of adolescence and competition. By the time lunch was over, they were friends.

- *Turn your shame into guilt.* At first glance this may not seem to be an improvement. But before you reject this option, consider guilt in relationship to shame. With guilt, we can feel deep pain, but we can make amends and get on with our lives. The sense of defectiveness and fundamental unlovableness that we feel with shame keeps us swamped in a downward spiral of immobilizing feelings — helplessness, hopelessness, despair, self-loathing.

> **Cary Ann** was handed a loaf of her mother-in-law's fresh-baked bread to slice for dinner. Embarrassed to admit that she had never sliced bread before, Cary Ann fumbled as she made an attempt. She had made two cuts with the knife when her mother-in-law looked over and said sharply, "Don't you know how to slice bread?" Cary Ann felt ashamed, exposed as ignorant, defective as a person because she couldn't measure up in the bread-slicing department.

In a situation like this, many of us might have answered, "What do you expect? This bread is too soft!" (Shame makes us experts in the art of the counterattack.) Some of us might have said, "Keep your damned bread!" before throwing the knife down and walking away.

> **Cary Ann** looked at her mother-in-law. Indeed, she was "guilty" of ignorance about slicing bread. Despite her embarrassment, she admitted her ignorance, saying, "I've never done this before. I didn't realize what a trick there is to it." By turning her shame into guilt, Cary Ann made amends for her ignorance (in this case, an apology was adequate) and got on with her life.

- *Substitute "guilty" for "ashamed" in your self-talk.* For example: "I'm ashamed of my big thighs" becomes "I'm guilty of having big thighs." The logical next step is to ask yourself, "How can I make amends for my big thighs?"

> When **Candi** asked herself that question, she burst into laughter. "I don't have to make amends for my body!" she proclaimed. "It just is!"

Another person might have said, "I can make amends by starting the diet I've been putting off for months." Still another might decide to start walking or working out. Almost any response to this question is bound to be positive.

Now consider this statement: "I am so ashamed. I don't deserve to have good things happen to me."

> When **Paul** did this exercise and substituted "guilty" for "ashamed" — "I am so guilty. I don't deserve to have good things happen to me" — he visibly bristled. "I don't need to make amends for that," he said. "Of course I deserve to have good things happen!"

This technique works, but use it wisely. Guilt can seem overwhelming and debilitating when we have been responsible for an accident because we drove carelessly or have severely abused someone. However, agonizing in our guilt cannot undo the harm we have done. Ways can be found to make amends — perhaps through volunteer work or helping others.

When shame and guilt occur simultaneously, turning shame into guilt may seem redundant. Again, we can make amends for guilt; shame can keep us swamped in hopelessness which makes change more difficult. Remember, too, that making amends is not a quick way to absolve ourselves from guilt. Rather, it is a first step toward healing relationships.

Consider the man who has repeatedly beaten his wife. He feels both shame and guilt. He has stopped the beatings and is trying to make amends for his violent behavior. This doesn't mean that his relationship with his wife will heal, or that his guilt will go away. It doesn't mean that his wife will feel the way he wants her to feel. The purpose of making amends isn't to "fix" something or someone else. The purpose of making amends is to start your own healing.

In an extreme situation such as family violence, the impact of shame-related behavior is so profound that everyone involved — the batterer, the victims, the witnesses — feels his or her own shame. Each one can take responsibility only for his or her own healing. It's tempting to believe that everything will be all right once "someone else" changes his or her behavior, but that simply isn't true. Victims continue to carry emotional wounds long after the violence has stopped and the batterer has sincerely tried to make amends.

The Positive Power of Laughter

Laughter is one of the purest, most powerful sources of genuine relief. The ability to laugh at ourselves is considered a sign of mental health. Freudian psychoanalysts make a complicated explanation of how laughter "redistributes psychic energy" which "dispels shame." For most of us, it's enough to know instinctively that laughter makes us feel good.

Of course we're not talking here about laughter at someone else's expense. That kind of laughter is cruel, an expression of hostility and aggressiveness. The laughter that brings genuine relief is simply another way that unexpectedness affects our lives.

As shame is connected to the feeling of being suddenly and unexpectedly exposed, laughter is linked to the surprise of a punchline, a tickle, a new way of looking at things. It can help us to arrive at a new way of looking at shame.

Over and over, people who attend 12-Step support groups say, "I thought I'd come here and we would all cry together. Instead, we're laughing about situations we feel terrible about. I don't understand!" We have learned to look at our situation in a new way. The laughter comes from our innate human ability to stand back, observe ourselves, and judge ourselves absurd. It's one of the very best healers of shame. How good it feels to laugh!

Genuine relief — that instant of harmony with ourselves and our world — can give us the strength to break away from the shame-anxiety cycle. It can give us the confidence to stop believing that we deserve the bad or don't deserve the good, and to start making positive changes in our lives.

CHAPTER NINE
EMOTIONAL CONSEQUENCES

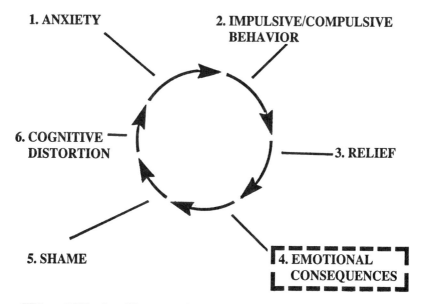

1. ANXIETY

2. IMPULSIVE/COMPULSIVE BEHAVIOR

6. COGNITIVE DISTORTION

3. RELIEF

5. SHAME

4. EMOTIONAL CONSEQUENCES

The High Cost of Relief

Our feeling of relief is quickly followed by a flood of uncomfortable feelings including guilt, hurt, remorse, distress, grief, inadequacy, rejection, disappointment, and anger. By the very nature of the shame-anxiety cycle, we will once again find ourselves facing the consequences of thoughts, feelings, and behaviors that have violated ourselves or others. How we deal with this flood of feelings plays an important role in our healing.

Bryan's anxiety grew as he struggled to understand what was happening to his marriage. Nothing he did or said seemed to be good enough for his wife. She spent most evenings out with her friends, leaving Bryan to baby-sit her two children. And when she was home she criticized him because he didn't make enough money. When they argued, which they often did, Bryan's anger quickly escalated into violence against things that he cared for. On separate occasions, he kicked in his car door, tore up his stereo speakers, threw the turntable across the room, shattered a picture of his daughter. For a few brief moments after each episode, he always felt "good" because his pent-up anxiety had been released. Then he plunged into acute depression for days.

When anxiety-driven behavior is this destructive, the damage to property is obvious. The damage to our self-concept is often not so visible. In Bryan's case, the resulting depression and remorse were apparent to himself and others. His wife would insist, "If you could just control yourself you wouldn't have to feel like this!"

For others, emotional flooding is not so apparent. In fact, we can become very adept at covering up the sweeping despair that many of us feel following impulsive/compulsive behaviors and the elusive period of relief.

For most of us, having Dad fix a meal is a treat. In **Jerome's** case, it was just one more way of exercising control over his family's eating habits, which he considered "abysmal." Each meal was accompanied by his lecture about how "his way" of meal planning was the best — the implication being that the others were too stupid and uncaring to eat right. Each meal was also accompanied by his wife's resentment and humiliation, his children's anxiety and fear of an outright battle between their parents.

The emotional consequences for Jerome were less apparent. Realizing that his controlling behavior was alienating him from his family, knowing that it was futile in terms of actually changing their eating behaviors, Jerome would groan inwardly as he felt his separation, inadequacy, and frustration. Meanwhile he would put on a "tough-guy" front, telling himself and acting as though it didn't matter that his efforts went unappreciated.

It is sometimes impossible to see the anguish of emotional consequences. Consider this case of the "perfect couple."

The friends of **Danny and Colleen** often commented, "They never fight." In fact, they used television to avoid intimacy, arguments, and each other.

Whenever Danny sensed tension in the relationship, he headed for the T.V. As he focused on the set, he blamed himself for the problems between him and Colleen. Finally rousing himself when the local station went off the air, he felt guilty because he hadn't spent any time with the kids that evening.

Meanwhile Colleen worried because she and Danny never brought issues out into the open. Seeing him in front of the T.V., she felt justified in joining him — "if he can sit there and relax, so can I!" Later she was swamped with feelings of regret at having spent yet another night in front of the TV.

Both Danny and Colleen gained immediate, if temporary, relief from their anxiety — reinforcement that kept them coming back for more despite their feelings of guilt and regret. Both lost in terms of their relationship with each other and their children.

Rhonda was a soft touch for every committee at her church. She had high expectations for herself in her role as a "valuable church member" and was very competent at whatever she did. Whenever she was asked to serve on still another committee, she would decline at first, realizing that she was already overbooked. The demands of her job were heavy; her husband and three young children needed her; she was taking graduate-level college courses. Then, as the chairperson described how important the committee was, Rhonda would start to feel anxious. She would impulsively agree to serve and immediately feel relief. But as soon as she hung up the phone, dismay would set in — "How can I find the time to do that?" This would be followed by anger — "I don't understand why they won't take no for an answer!" She would promise herself never to serve on another committee, and she would stick to her promise until the next time she was asked.

Rhonda believed that she didn't deserve to set her own limits. This irrational belief raised her anxiety to the point where she sought relief by impulsively agreeing to do a job she didn't want to do. Afterward she was flooded with painful emotional consequences, anger directed at "those people who put me on the spot" and at herself because "I can't say no." Despite her many talents and her commitment to her church, Rhonda found herself in conflict about her obligations most of the time.

Interrupting the Emotional Consequences

Recall that the phases of the shame-anxiety cycle are not so clear in real life as they are in the illustration. They can happen instantaneously and simultaneously. We are usually not aware that we're moving from one phase to another, or even that we're caught in a self-destructive cycle.

Becoming aware of our feelings is a first step toward breaking free. This brings us once again to the role denial and minimization play in fueling the shame-anxiety cycle.

Denial and Minimization

So far we have described denial and minimization only in negative terms. Dr. Elisabeth Kübler-Ross, writing about grief and loss, makes the point that denial and minimization have value when used in moderation. She identifies denial as a first, predictable stage in adjusting to the sorrows in our life. It softens the blow, allowing information to seep into our conscious minds when we are ready to absorb it. Denial becomes a problem only when it becomes a habit, when we use it constantly to avoid facing the consequences of our own behavior or the behavior of others.

There's a reason why we feel the vast array of emotions we do. When we behave in a way that violates our core self or others' (or when our core self is violated by someone else), our anger, guilt, grief, dismay, disappointment, inadequacy, and so on act as signals. They let us know that our own or someone else's behavior is not acceptable, that our environment is not safe. If we pay attention, our feelings can guide us in correcting or changing our behavior or environment or challenging the behavior of another who violates us.

Many people find these feelings so uncomfortable that they minimize or stuff them. Maybe you've said to someone, "You look tired," and had them respond, "No, not really," when it was obvious that they could barely drag one foot after another. Or maybe someone has asked you, "Are you angry?" and you've shaken your head and said, "Not really," when in fact you were furious. Later you may have thought to yourself, "Why did I say that? I *was* angry!"

There's an important distinction between the conscious choice to protect yourself and the reflexive, unconscious use of denial and minimization. We all have the right to guard our own boundaries. When others push to know more about us than we want them to know, or to take more of us than we want to give, we have the right to raise our defenses.

> **Gene** beamed as he reported the results of a dreaded inspection by his supervisor. "I stood up to him!" he said. "For the first time in five years on the job, I stood up for myself! As usual, he started criticizing the minute he came into my office. He'd 'noticed I hadn't put in quite as many hours last month.' I just told him that I was feeling very satisfied with last month's record because I had increased sales by 7 percent. And, you know what, he just blinked and didn't say another critical thing!"

People who habitually deny their feelings (or whose feelings are denied by others) may seem to "forget" that they even have feelings — especially feelings considered unacceptable by those around them. For example: A woman who is ridiculed by her husband in front of friends protests his behavior, and not for the first time. He discounts her feelings by responding, "You just don't have any sense of humor!" She discounts her own feelings, telling herself, "Well, it wasn't that big a deal."

Or consider the child whose father promises to take him to the zoo, then doesn't appear. This sort of thing has happened often since his parents divorced. The child might think, "Daddy must have forgotten" — denying his own disappointment, denying that his father has acted irresponsibly.

In fact, making excuses for ourselves or for others is a clear sign that we are denying and minimizing.

Making Excuses

Excuses are different from reasons. Reasons exist in reality. Sometimes these things happen. Sometimes parents forget promises to their children. Sometimes the Dannys and Colleens of the world watch TV when they could be talking. Sometimes the Rhondas of the world overextend themselves. Sometimes it rains in California.

Excuses are a product of denial and minimization. They present an illusion of reality. We "make excuses" — manufacture them out of our shame-based fear of revealing ourselves or others for what or who we really are. Making excuses to others and to ourselves is usually a way to protect ourselves from the emotional consequences of either their behaviors or ours.

We cover for ourselves, saying, like Jerome, "I'm just trying to help my family stay healthy" — an effort to avoid facing his family's resentment and anxiety. Or we maintain, "I hit every stop light in town," afraid to admit that we overslept again. "My wife will be really angry if I'm late for dinner," we state, in an indirect effort to protect ourselves from a demanding supervisor.

We cover for others. "He works really hard and needs a chance to relax," says Colleen in defense of Danny's television habit, when one of her friends is critical. "I slipped and hit the corner of the coffee table," claims Edie after her husband blackens her eye, not wanting to reveal her embarrassment and fear. "It runs in the family. My sister was the same way," we say about our child's temper tantrum, hiding our frustration.

Tools and Techniques for Interrupting the Emotional Consequences

Denial, minimization, and excuses all keep us from being aware of our feelings — the emotional consequences of our impulsive/compulsive behavior. It is difficult, perhaps even impossible, to heal until we begin to face the reality of our own feelings.

Becoming more aware of our feelings is a three-step process. The first step involves *finding* our feelings — digging down into our garbage bag and pulling them out. The second step is *identifying* the feelings, or naming them. The third step is *expressing* the feelings to ourselves and others.

Finding the Feelings

There is a simple exercise you can do to "get in touch" with your feelings. The goal is to focus on your physical sensations — the way your body feels — rather than your emotions.

1. Go to a quiet place where you're not likely to be interrupted.

2. Get comfortable, then "listen" to your body. Start with your toes and work up, or start with your head and work down. Pay attention to the tiniest details.

3. Now describe your body's feelings to yourself out loud. For example: "I can feel the tightness of my shirt cuffs on my wrists . . . . It feels as though they have rubbed a little. My skin feels tender." Or: "My legs are feeling trembly. I've been rushing around today and I can feel the quivers in the muscles." (Don't worry about sounding silly; who's around to hear you?)

4. Repeat steps 1–3 once a day, three days in a row.

Many people who try this exercise for the first time become very anxious and want to quit because they can't "do it right." They are so used to denying their physical (and emotional) sensations that they can't even find the feelings — what's happening to their bodies — much less put their feelings into words. If you have problems with this exercise, you may be doing some stuffing of your own.

What do you say when someone asks you, "How are you today?" Do you quickly respond "I don't know yet," "Oh, I'm here," or "Fine," despite the fact that your head has been throbbing since breakfast? Do you sometimes feel ravenously hungry all of a sudden only to realize that you haven't eaten all day? These are ways we deny our body signals. As you practice the exercise, you will become more aware of your own.

Naming the Feelings

Many people have a hard time putting words to their feelings. They have been denying or minimizing so habitually and for so long that they simply lack a vocabulary beyond the basics — "upset," "happy," "sad," "angry," "bored," "confused." Others may have come from an environment where people didn't talk about feelings. Whatever the cause, an inability to identify and express a broader spectrum of feelings leads to a diminished sense of self.

The lists below are meant to serve as starting points for naming feelings. Each begins with one of the basic feelings and moves from less intense to more powerful ones.

Upset	*Happy*	*Sad*
Bothered	Glad	Sorry
Uneasy	Pleased	Deflated
Nervous	Cheerful	Distressed
Shaken	Delighted	Disheartened
Flustered	Optimistic	Disappointed
Defensive	Joyful	Discouraged
Apprehensive	Thrilled	Dejected
Desperate	Jubilant	Hurt
Inadequate	Elated	Devastated
Anxious		

Angry	*Bored*	*Confused*
Displeased	Tolerant	Undecided
Annoyed	Resigned	Uncomfortable
Aggravated	Disenchanted	Uncertain
Perturbed	Stifled	Troubled
Irritated	Reluctant	Hesitant
Resentful	Guarded	Perplexed
Mad	Uneasy	Ambivalent
Fuming	Stagnant	Disorganized
Furious	Constricted	Helpless
Enraged	Apathetic	Immobilized

Help yourself to remember the words by reading the lists aloud. Look up definitions in a dictionary. Then choose one or two words from each list to add to your working (everyday) vocabulary. Practice saying them and imagine times when you might want to use them. For reinforcement, write them down on a piece of paper and carry it with you.

When **Carla** was raped by her cousin Mark, a man she had known and trusted since childhood, she was incapable of identifying and expressing the betrayal, terror, grief, and devastation she felt. Several months into counseling, she received an early-morning obscene phone call from a man who said he had been following her and watching her. At first Carla feared that she would fall apart. She had just begun to heal, and she felt devastated by this new violation.

As she progressed in her healing, she was asked how she was able to get back into recovery. "Oh, that's easy!" she exclaimed. "This time I talked, and talked, and talked about my feelings. They just came out. Pop! Pop! Pop! I was furious, enraged, teed off, and terrified, and I told people I felt that way. I don't think I've ever talked about my feelings like that before."

Expressing the Feelings

Once we find our feelings and name them, we can begin to express them. This exercise can show you how.

1. Choose one of the wordlists on page 81. Now pick one of the words near the top of the column (for example, "annoyed" for angry, "uncomfortable" for confused).

2. Say to yourself, under your breath, "I feel _____," and fill in the blank with the word you chose in step 1.

   Don't be surprised if this feels awkward. You may even experience physical sensations in response to the feeling word statement. (For every emotion, there is a related physical feeling.) For example: Saying "I feel displeased," you may be aware of a corresponding tightening in parts of your body. Saying "I feel glad" is likely to result in a loosening and warming sensation. As you become more comfortable with feeling word statements, you may find yourself remembering or visualizing situations in which you felt the emotion you are saying.

3. Once you are comfortable with making the "I feel _____" statement under your breath, try saying it aloud.

   This will feel foolish at first but will become less so with practice. Give yourself time. Practice several statements each day, under your breath if necessary. It may take weeks or an entire month to master this step.

4. Finally, say your "I feel _____" statement aloud to someone else.

   Children are generally safe to practice on. Or you may decide to risk this with a close friend. Don't expect yourself to go any further. And don't expect others to respond to your feeling statement by "taking care of" or fixing your feelings.

The "I Message"

When you reach the point where you're comfortable saying "I feel _____" to someone else, it's time to move on to a full-fledged "I message."

An "I message" is one of the most effective ways to express oneself. Basically, it has three parts:

1. I feel . . .
2. Because . . . or When . . . , and
3. I'd like . . .

For example:

1. I feel very frightened . . .
2. . . . because you are driving so fast on this gravel road and . . .
3. . . . I'd like you to slow down a little.

Or:

1. I feel very concerned . . .
2. . . . when I hear you talk about quitting your job and . . .
3. . . . I'd like to know more about your plans.

The "I message" is effective because you are taking responsibility for only your own feelings. Sometimes other people will attempt to deny your feelings, saying things like, "Oh, you don't have to worry." The fact is — and the "I message" makes it abundantly clear — that we feel what we feel. There is no "right" or "wrong" to feelings. The behavior that comes from our feelings can be called "appropriate" or "inappropriate," but not the feelings themselves. Therefore we don't have to defend an "I message." It just is.

Practice using "I messages." Start with a neutral or safe statement — one you might make to someone you don't know well. Then move on to a more personal statement — one you might make to someone you work with. When you feel comfortable with these, try sending an "I message" to a close friend or loved one.

Getting Over Feeling Shy About "I"

You may feel shy at the very idea of starting a sentence with "I." Most of us have been carefully taught not to put "I" first. You may remember running up to your mother to announce excitedly, "Me and Johnny caught three fish!" only to be told, "Never say 'me and Johnny.' Say 'Johnny and I.' Always put the other person first."

We've learned not to talk about ourselves in other ways, or people will perceive us as boasting or bragging: "Boy, Johnny is really on an ego trip!" "Tooting your own horn again?" It's no wonder we're cautious!

However, if we really want to make a genuine connection with another person, we need to let them know "who" we are. "I messages" eliminate the guesswork in our relationships. By revealing ourselves and our feelings, we remove the barriers between ourselves and others.

Feel, Think, Believe

Many of us have difficulty distinguishing what we feel from what we think or believe. Often we use the word "feel" as a synonym for "think" or "believe" — another way we unconsciously mask the reality of our feeling responses.

Beginners who are trying to learn to use "I messages" will say things like, "I feel you should quit jumping on the bed." Here the word "feel" is not about the speaker's emotions. It is about what he or she thinks or believes about jumping on beds. It becomes a "you message," and "you messages" are almost always blaming, attacking, or commanding. They have a tendency to raise barriers between people.

One way to check out the feeling part of "I messages" is to substitute the words "think" or "believe" for the word "feel." If what you are expressing really isn't a feeling, either will sound all right in the sentence. For example, it makes sense to say, "I think that you should quit jumping on the bed." It doesn't make sense to say, "I think angry when I see you jump on the bed." The sentence clicks when you say, "I feel angry when I see you jump on the bed, and I want you to stop."

Shame and "I Messages"

Our sense of shame interferes with our ability to express ourselves through "I messages." We discount our value to others when we believe "They wouldn't care anyway" (with its hidden message, "I don't deserve to have them care"). We hesitate to expose ourselves, our wants or needs. Or, as one of my clients said, "I wouldn't want them to be with me just because I needed them." Sometimes we are so ashamed of our wants and needs, and have been ashamed for so long, that it's almost impossible to complete an "I message" because we hardly know ourselves what we would like to have happen!

There are times when we want to protect ourselves from exposure and violation by choosing not to reveal ourselves. We may also choose to be direct about expressing our limits. Here again, an "I message" is the ideal medium. "I don't want to talk about that now because it's too personal," we can say. "I'd like to have you drop the subject." Others may ridicule our desire for privacy or feel uncomfortable about our directness, especially if they are accustomed to our being doormats for them. We may find this intimidating or discouraging, but neither diminishes the value of what we have said.

We have the right to express our feelings. We don't have the right to expect others to like what they hear, or to meet our needs just because we have expressed them. The "I message" makes clear what is going on with us. It gives others information they need to decide how to relate to us. Their responses give us information about where we stand with them.

More Benefits of "I Messages"

"I messages" also affect and define our relationship to ourselves. When we strive to accurately identify and express our feelings, we are also affirming our view of reality to ourselves. As noted earlier, it hurts when others deny or discount our reality. It hurts even more, and causes even greater damage to our sense of self, when we deny, minimize, or camouflage our own feelings about what we're experiencing. Using "I messages" is an excellent way to get in touch and stay in touch with ourselves.

The value of "I messages" is not measured by how others respond to them. In fact, focusing on this can sidetrack us from the primary purpose of facing our feelings. When we express ourselves clearly, we feel genuinely happy, peaceful, or contented because we are no longer denying our core selves and our reality. We have begun to change ourselves, to move closer to our sense of who and what we can be.

I once saw a poster that read, "It's easier to stay out than get out." Similarly, "staying out" of the shame-anxiety cycle by dealing with our feelings is easier than struggling to "get out" from under the pressure of the flywheel. One frees our energy; the other consumes it.

The Value of Tears

How long has it been since you cried — really cried? Many people find it difficult or embarrassing, even impossible to cry. Much of this is due to early learning: parental admonitions like "Don't be such a crybaby!" or threats like "If you keep up that crying, I'll give you something to cry about," and even "You keep on crying and you're going to the orphanage!"

For some children, the ability to hold back tears is the only way to resist brutalization: "At least I didn't give them the satisfaction of crying." Whatever its origin, the stigma of crying is hard to overcome. Sometimes it feels as if we've pushed down so much pain and discouragement that we would cry forever if we let ourselves start.

Crying can be a sign that healing is taking place. Often the tears signify our growing ability to face the reality of our pain, either in the present or from the past. Crying can also promote our healing. We talk about "crying it out," a confirmation that our tears can carry our pain away.

If you have found yourself "weeping over the littlest things," your tears are still a validation of the pain you carry. In this case, I suspect, we cry for others from an unconscious belief that it is not okay for us to cry for ourselves — that we don't deserve it.

No matter how we express our emotional distress, for shame-based people the ability to cry for ourselves is a signal that we are beginning to believe we are worthy of tears. That in itself is a positive change.

Dealing with Anger

In Chapter Two we looked at the shame-anger connection and learned that anger is often a secondary feeling that protects us from the pain of a primary feeling. If we focus on the negative aspects of anger and try to "control it," as many people do, we maintain any problems relating to our anger because we don't get to the underlying painful feelings.

One reason why we have difficulty "handling" anger is our confusion between the feeling and the behaviors connected to it. Like other emotions, anger is neither "bad" nor "good." Our anger simply is. Anger becomes a problem only when it is too intense, last too long, or begins to disrupt relationships.

The intensity of our anger is often tied to acting out in a destructive way, as Bryan did when he destroyed his own possessions. We may attack others verbally and physically. If our anger hangs on, there can be severe physical consequences: high blood pressure, ulcers, headaches, muscle pains, and other stress-related illnesses. When our anger begins to disrupt relationships we are left feeling isolated, even abandoned, which increases our susceptibility to entrapment in the shame-anxiety cycle.

Our uncomfortable relationship with anger is evident in the words we use to give ourselves permission to feel it: "justifiable anger." But this is a contradiction in terms. Anger is; we don't have to justify its existence. The source of our anger is irrelevant. We may have been victimized in the past. We may be violated in the present. What matters is the effect anger has on our lives at this point. Like acid, anger eats away at the vessel that contains it, asking not whether it is justified in doing so.

I often become angry as I watch survivors of brutalization struggle with their wrenching emotional trauma. My anger is not with them, but for them. It is as though they have been victimized twice—first, in the original trauma; secondly, in the agony of facing the consequences of the violation. Part of the healing process is dealing with the anger — whether it is explosive (directed outward) or implosive (directed inward or stuffed).

We often stuff our anger. We deny its existence even in situations where not to be angry would be out of touch with reality. We have the right to face our anger honestly and deal with it directly. We also have the right to set our own pace for peeling away the anger and facing the sensitive feelings our anger conceals.

Tools and Techniques for Dealing with Anger

If we are in the habit of venting our anger in destructive ways through verbal or physical abusiveness or violence, it is very important to interrupt those behaviors. It is exceedingly difficult to deal with the underlying anger until the destructiveness is halted.

As with other impulsive/compulsive behaviors, one of the most effective ways to interrupt destructive anger-related behavior is the time-out, a technique described on pages 61-62.

Other constructive ways to address anger issues include finding, naming, and expressing our feelings verbally rather than physically, as described earlier in this chapter — a healthy alternative to stuffing them. We can use "I messages" to tell others how we feel without taking our feelings out on them.

Or we can discharge our anger in ways that won't harm anyone. Here are some ideas to consider:

- Go for a walk or a run. Getting oxygen into your system will help clean out the extra adrenaline released by the "fight or flight" response, a primitive, instinctive reaction to intense feelings of anger. If you can't exercise, do some deep breathing. Oxygen calms your mind and body.

- Roll a newspaper into a "bat." Use it to strike or hit against some solid object that can't be damaged—a sturdy table or counter, a doorframe, a bench in the garage, an upright brace in the basement. As your "bat" disintegrates, some of your anger will dissipate.

- Take a fairly solid cardboard box to a safe place, then kick it. Or pick up the box and throw it against a wall or onto the floor.

- Pound on your pillow or bed — a way to meet resistance without danger to yourself. Feel the satisfaction of releasing your physical and emotional impulses.

- Tear up a newspaper. Rip it to shreds, into chunks, whatever you choose. Cleaning up after yourself can symbolize "dumping" your anger.

A few words of caution about hitting, kicking, pounding, and tearing activities: If you usually act out your anger through violence, these activities could feed into that and make you even more angry. And you could frighten or intimidate the people around you who have already experienced your violent or threatening behavior. To them, it will look like more of the same. Take a time-out instead.

- Don't do any activity that ordinarily requires caution, like chopping wood, riding a bicycle or motorcycle, driving a car, or operating dangerous equipment. Anger impairs judgment. Don't take the chance of hurting yourself or someone else.

As you face and deal with your anger, you may feel the strong urge to cry. In a sense, it's like peeling an onion: peel away the anger, and the primary, painful feeling comes to the surface. It doesn't feel good, but it's real. Let yourself cry about it.

Finally, here are two relatively quiet and peaceful ways to deal with anger. For those of us who aren't comfortable with or capable of "getting physical," these alternatives also work well.

- Log your anger. Get it out, write it down, leave it on paper. Then put it away and come back to it later. Soon you will begin to see patterns to your anger — situations that usually evoke your anger response; things you typically think about when you're angry. Use this information and insight to make new choices and changes.

One of my clients used a spiral notebook which she dubbed "My Mad Book." She would identify her anger, express it in a number of different ways, and briefly describe the situation. For example:

Monday, 7:00 p.m.

I'm mad—mad—MAD. The kids started bickering at supper again tonight and I couldn't get them to stop. I sat with them for a while but began to feel my anger heating up so I told them I was going to take a time-out and walked around the block. When I came back I talked with them and found out they had forgotten what they were even fighting about. It feels like I took it too seriously

• Take a "feeling break." Often we deal with our feelings like Scarlett O'Hara; we put off thinking about them until "tomorrow." Only tomorrow never comes. Today — right now, if possible — take 15 minutes for yourself. Set a timer or alarm clock, then sit down by yourself and let yourself feel. Don't make up reasons why you shouldn't feel the way you do. Don't use the time to worry or plan; don't distract yourself from the purpose of your break. Just feel. You may want to refer to your feeling word list to help identify and express your emotional state.

CHAPTER TEN

SHAME

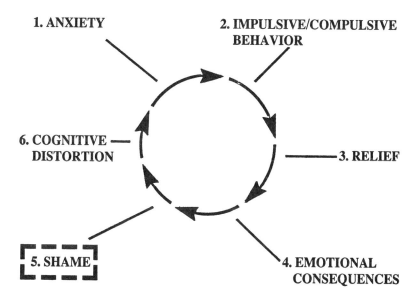

1. ANXIETY

2. IMPULSIVE/COMPULSIVE BEHAVIOR

6. COGNITIVE DISTORTION

3. RELIEF

5. SHAME

4. EMOTIONAL CONSEQUENCES

Transformation Through Shame

Because shame elicits such strong feelings of mortification, embarrassment, and humiliation, it's easy to lose sight of the helpful side of shame. Shame's positive power can move us to change, to aim for the stars, to try to be the best we can be. This power for transformation seems to be related to our core-self ability to:

- know a finer way of being, and
- observe and evaluate our efforts to be more self-creating, self-directing, in harmony with ourselves and our world.

> **Wesley** tells of the moment he knew his life had to change. As he carried another drink back to his table in the crowded, impersonal bar, he was struck by the thought, "There has to be more to life than this!" he realized that he was thirsting for more than the satisfaction of his physical needs. He wanted to be connected to others, giving and receiving love to his fullest capacity.

Like Wesley, we are actors on the stage of life, going through the motions, doing what we believe is the best (sometimes the only) thing we can do in our own situations. We also are observers, drama critics who watch the action, critique our performance, and offer suggestions for improvement.

With shame, as with the tension that exists between actors and drama critics, there can be a split between what we can do and what we actually do. Especially if we are operating out of a shame base, this split seems to create a world of opposites where we see either/or, black/white, right/wrong, good/bad. We know we have good within us; we believe we are bad. We want to bring our secrets out into the open; we fear to reveal ourselves.

> **Ryan** wanted to ask his wife's help to deal with a stressful situation on the job, but at the same time he believed that he didn't deserve her help. "My self-esteem is so low," he explained." "I want Elizabeth to know what is happening to me, but I'm afraid she'll kick me out if she knows just how much I've screwed up at work. I can't even face her in my imagination. I pictured myself covering my face and hiding in a corner. I realized that even this wasn't enough. What I really wanted was to be able to hide in a box — completely covered — and plead with her from there."

If we have been living in a world of extremes, split into "okay/not okay" thinking, we will probably be unduly harsh in our self-imposed judgments. We may find ourselves being punitive rather than learning from our mistakes. Like Ryan, we may believe we don't deserve the good, yet realize deep down inside that this is not the way we want our lives to be.

Our ability to conceptualize another, more satisfying way to live is as much a quality of shame as the harshness. Shame makes it possible to know simultaneously what being okay is about, as well as knowing when we are not okay. Very often, in our pain, we fail to recognize how our capacity to know what is good can keep alive a tiny flicker of hope, fueling our desire for harmony and union. Ironically, we could not know despair if we did not also have the capability to feel hope.

Philosopher Herbert Morris captures the hurtful capacity in his statement, "Shame is the defeat . . . of love." Shame can isolate us from others and from our core selves. Psychoanalyst Helen Merrell Lynd argues that shame also carries the power for "transformation of the self." In this chapter we will build on the power of shame to transform us into self-regulating, loving individuals with a sense of compassion and justice.

The Value of "Selfishness"

When we believe we don't deserve the good, this hampers our ability to take care of ourselves. We wait for others to satisfy our needs, labeling ourselves "selfish" or "self-centered" if we tend to them on our own. This sets the stage for dependence, anxiety, and anger. Here is how this process appears to function:

1. We have a need, want, or desire.

2. Believing that we don't deserve to take care of our need, want, or desire, we depend on someone or something outside ourselves to satisfy it. We wait for a parent, spouse, lover or friend to "make us feel better." Or we turn to alcohol/other drugs, gambling, food, sex, and so on to "make us feel good."

3. If it's people we depend on, we expect them to know what we need without our telling them. "If they really loved me," we think, "they would know without being told. If I have to tell them, that means they don't really care."

4. The people who love us do try. Or the alcohol/other drugs, gambling, food, sex, and so on perform their function.

5. But we still don't feel good. Because we haven't identified or expressed our need, the "fix" fails to satisfy.

6. We become angry, maybe even enraged, that our need hasn't been met. We depended on that someone or something! We still feel worthless, bad, hopeless, unlovable.

Even if we experience some temporary satisfaction, it isn't genuine. Our core self knows that depending on others to satisfy our needs is not being true to ourselves. It knows that we're capable of making our own choices and setting our own course. When we expect someone or something else to satisfy our needs, we are denying our core self.

Shame and Core-Self Denial

I believe that core-self denial is a critical contributing factor toward entrapment in the swamp of shame. The act of core-self denial seems to trigger a deep, fundamental conflict between our "knowing" part and our "observing" part.

Consider the child who has a quarter to put in the Sunday School collection plate. Part of her wants to keep the quarter to spend on candy; part wants to give it to the church, as was intended. If something like this has ever happened to you, then you are well aware of the switching from side to side, the internal argument we often term "wrestling with our conscience." We know this debate may go on until the moment our hand is poised over the collection plate. Will I? Won't I? Should I? Shouldn't I?

Our ability to engage in this moral, ethical debate (both within ourselves and with others) is, to me, one of the greatest gifts we receive from our ability to feel shame. Ironically, because of the splitting nature of shame, it can also become one of the strongest negative features of shame.

When our shame response is extreme, the internal debate seems to be correspondingly intense or rigorous. Our ability to love ourselves, to nurture ourselves, protect ourselves, and self-direct our drive to mature is immobilized. When we act or are acted upon in ways that are self-destructive rather than self-constructive, we find ourselves hampered in our ability to change. As we vacillate between the alternatives — between the good/bad, right/wrong, either/or — much of our energy is consumed in the conflict.

If we typically use denial to deal with our life problems, it is predictable that we will turn to denial here, in this case to denial of our core self. We become stuck in the shame-based beliefs that we deserve the bad or don't deserve the good. We deny our own love and acceptance to our own selves.

Marea gave me the most explicit example of this internal debate. As she talked about her desire to end her life — thus her pain — by suicide, she shared the contempt she felt for herself: "You might as well betray yourself," she said. "You've betrayed everyone else."

Sometimes we get so out of touch with our core selves that we lose any sense of who we really are. We feel empty inside, hollow. We crave love and affection so much that we may settle for cheap imitations, then find ourselves even more disappointed and hurting.

We "believe" the person we meet at the singles bar who tells us that we're the one he or she has been waiting for. We "fake" the kind of person we think others expect us to be in an effort to win their approval. We bend ourselves into emotional pretzels, convinced that if we wear the right clothes, drink the right beer, use the right deodorant, drive the right car, everything will be okay.

Instead, we find a hollow victory. We may "get" the guy or the gal, but our life is a sham as we keep hiding our true selves. This continuing denial of our core selves fuels the shame-anxiety cycle.

We behave the way we think "they" want us to. We allow others (persons, objects, alcohol/other drugs) to take control of our lives. We are flooded with feelings of discouragement and self-betrayal. We feel ashamed, exposed to our watching core self as "less than." Our thinking is distorted. We believe that we don't deserve to have life be more genuinely satisfying. We become anxious and afraid of the impostor we have become, pretending to be what we really aren't. We perform some impulsive/compulsive behavior or let someone else walk all over us. We are trapped in the shame-anxiety cycle.

Exercises in self-love, self-acceptance, and self-nurturing are effective ways to activate the transforming power of shame. It can be exceedingly difficult to begin this process if you are accustomed to denying your core self. Begin slowly, one baby step at a time. The following tools and techniques are designed to help.

Tools and Techniques for Overcoming Core-Self Denial

Any 12-Step program participant will recognize this saying: *Be good to yourself.* This doesn't mean to recklessly indulge yourself or focus only on yourself. Instead, it means to be the kind of person who is capable of behaving, thinking, and believing in such a way that your core self feels good about the way you conduct your life. It means being as kind, affirming, forgiving, accepting, and giving to yourself as you like to be toward others. It means taking care of yourself physically, intellectually, emotionally, and spiritually.

Here is how **Pat** explained his understanding of "be good to yourself": "I wanted a milkshake this afternoon. As I was considering whether I should have one or not, I decided I would, thinking, 'Why not be good to myself?' Then I realized that the best thing I could do for myself was to not take on any more calories, because I really do want to lose some weight."

Following are some other suggested ways to be good to yourself. Before you start, designate a small notebook your "log book." Use it to record your intentions and make real your commitment; to track your progress; to identify patterns or problem areas.

- *Be good to yourself physically:* Take a walk. Do some stretching exercises. Soak in a warm tub while you listen to your favorite music. Get a manicure, haircut, or massage.

- *Be good to yourself intellectually:* Read a chapter in a book that you value. Listen to a talk show on public radio. Read an editorial in the newspaper. Write a letter. Stretch your mind by listening to and affirming another person's point of view, even if you don't agree. Ask your kids what they studied in school today, and let them teach you.

- *Be good to yourself emotionally:* Write a poem about your feelings. Cuddle a new baby. Ask someone for a hug. Allow yourself to cry. Smile at someone you don't know. Accept a compliment. Call a friend you've been lonely for.

- *Be good to yourself spiritually:* Stop by a church, chapel, or synagogue to pray. Take a few moments to meditate on an uplifting thought. Give yourself ten minutes of basking in the sunshine, being open to the sights, smells, and sounds around you. Read a scripture. Listen to refreshing music. Read a poem. Do a good deed without being found out.

If none of these suggestions seems right for you, seek or invent others. First, however, ask yourself why you find them unacceptable. Maybe the very idea of being good to yourself is anxiety-provoking. Maybe you're accustomed to ignoring your needs. Maybe the thought of change is unsettling.

Try to do at least one small thing for yourself each day, despite your doubts or fears. Start slow and don't be hard on yourself if things don't work out according to plan.

Self-Nurturing Through Imaging

Imaging is an excellent self-nurturing tool. Following are two imaging exercises to practice on. If imaging works for you, check your local library or bookstore for books and audiotapes with more exercises. Or make your own audiotape, a personal guide to your favorite visualizations.

• *Happy Time*

Find a relatively quiet spot where you can make yourself comfortable. Close your eyes and let your memory drift back to a time when you felt happy, good about yourself, proud, filled with the glow of achievement. If nothing from your own past comes to mind, imagine a time when you felt happy for someone you loved. Or remember a warm and happy scene from a movie or TV show. Once you've chosen your happy time or scene, immerse yourself in it. Smell the smells; hear the sounds; feel the air around you. Linger as long as you want, then slowly return to the present, refreshed.

• *Nature Break*

Find a relatively quiet spot where you can make yourself comfortable. Close your eyes and imagine yourself in your favorite outdoor setting. Visualize yourself approaching the scene, feeling the anticipation, savoring the warm and cool of the sunshine and shadows. Allow yourself time to slowly settle into the image you've created; today there's no need to rush. In your imagination, you can give yourself all the time in the world. You are alone but not lonely. As you bask in the satisfaction and contentedness that you feel in your favorite spot, let your body and mind release all the tension you have brought with you. Feel it evaporate into the freshness of this world you have created in your mind. When you are restored to a state of well-being, slowly return to the present.

Building Interpersonal Bridges

A very important part of self-nurturing is the process of making connections with others: building interpersonal bridges. This involves either reaching out to others, responding to others who reach out to you, or both.

If you are feeling anxious about being the first one to speak, take comfort in the fact that many people you perceive as snobs or "not your type" may be reserved and withdrawn because they are just as shy and frightened as you are. Like you, they are waiting for someone else to break the ice; like you, they are wishing that they knew what to say and how to say it.

Even so-called "extroverts" and "gregarious" people appreciate it when someone else makes the first move. Many of them are highly anxious about social situations. Instead of withdrawing, they try to gain control (and contain their anxiety) by overextending themselves, and they may come off as blustering or overbearing. Don't let this "front" scare you away.

Eye Contact . . . and Beyond

Laid out below is a plan for how to build interpersonal bridges. It was developed by a group I was facilitating for adults who had problems with interpersonal relationships. They outlined their plan in small, manageable steps. They spent at least one week on each step, sometimes taking longer until they became comfortable with and confident about their social skills. Like them, start slowly, practicing each step as often as you deem necessary before you feel ready to proceed to the next.

1. Look at yourself in a mirror. Make eye contact with yourself and hold for a slow count of five. Increase gradually until you can maintain contact for a slow count of twenty.

2. Make eye contact with someone "safe," like a child or an elder. Keep it brief; a slow count of one is probably sufficient, since longer may feel uncomfortable for you and the other person. (Young children may be an exception to this because they haven't yet learned socially acceptable body language.) To limit others' visual access to you, consciously lower your eyes or break the gaze.

3. Make brief eye contact with a sales clerk at a check-out counter.

4. Make eye contact with a sales clerk and say "Hello" or "Thank you," whichever is appropriate.

5. Make eye contact with a sales clerk, say "Hello" or "Thank you," and add a socially acceptable, impersonal icebreaker such as "How do you like this weather?" "How are you today?" "Looks like it's pretty busy (or slow) today." Listen to others as they interact at the check-out counter to learn other appropriate phrases.

6. If your neighborhood feels like a place where you can do this safely, make brief eye contact with someone you meet on the street. Smile, if you're comfortable. If you're not comfortable, save the smile until you are.

7. Make eye contact with someone in a work or social setting (church, a concert) and smile.

8. Make eye contact with someone in a work or social setting, smile, and say "Hello."

9. Make eye contact with someone in a work or social setting, smile, say "Hello," and add a socially acceptable, impersonal icebreaker such as "How are things going?" "What's up?" "How are you?"

10. Be prepared for people to respond to you. Social activities are like tennis: You volley to them, they volley back, and it's up to you to be ready.

This process will not work with all of the people all of the time. Some will choose not to engage in any contact with you, period. That is their choice. Some will be as abrupt or unresponsive as you used to be. You can't change that. But unless your circumstances are highly unusual, you should be able to plan on receiving two responses for every three tries. And you'll start to feel more connected to others.

When **Herb** became state president of the Jaycees, he and his wife, Lori, began attending several banquets and social functions together. At first, she was miserable. Herb knew everyone, and she knew no one. Herb had responsibilities to tend to as part of his presidency, and she had nothing to do. After a month of trying to fade into the background, Lori used her embarrassment as a motivator for change. She took a crash course in conversational gambits. She read magazines and newspapers, watched the news religiously, and took notes to aid her memory. Soon she was returning from banquets and social functions with a glow of self-confidence, talking happily about the new friends she was making.

A few words of caution: At times our yearning to be connected can become so overwhelming that we unconsciously ask more than others are willing to give. When we find someone who responds positively, someone we feel safe with, we want even more of that "good stuff" called acceptance. We become a little like a traveler who has been lost in the desert; chancing on an oasis, we drink the well dry. Our neediness becomes greediness, and our greediness drives others away. As you start getting positive results from your efforts to create interpersonal bridges, remember to be moderate. Contact feels so wonderful that you may be tempted to tell more or ask more than is safe at the beginning of a friendship. And this can set the shame-anxiety cycle in motion all over again.

Avoiding the Caretaking Trap

Have you ever tried to cope with anxiety by "taking care" of a situation? This is a common response to feelings of inadequacy or shame. Unsure of what we should do, we offer to help the hostess; keep busy with little things; take care of others.

In the short run, caretaking helps us deal with anxiety. In the long run, it can be exhausting. Like Rhonda, who couldn't say no to church committees, we train others to expect us to be capable, responsible, and always available. That's fine for a while, and we gain social approval for being "such hard workers." Eventually, however, we crash and burn, filled with resentment and feeling like a martyr.

Others may say, "I had no idea you were feeling so bad! If only I'd known, I would have helped you." Believing we don't deserve to acknowledge our needs or have them met, it doesn't occur to us to ask for help or accept it when it's offered. We cut ourselves off from receiving nurturing and connectedness. We deny others the chance to be caregivers.

Carole's husband had been acutely depressed for two years. During that time, Carole had assumed his responsibilities as well as hers. At first she had tried asking him for help, but he always refused. Over time she learned to rely only on herself. She didn't realize how disconnected she was from others until she went to a family gathering. Several times over a two-day period, her cousin Robin offered to help with tasks that Carole was performing. Each time, Carole politely refused. As she was struggling down the sidewalk, burdened with heavy baggage, it suddenly struck her: "Why am I straining myself like this when Robin wants to help?" In that moment, she realized how cut off she was from the caring of others. She turned to her cousin with tears in her eyes and said, "I'm really sorry. I just realized how much you have offered to help, and how much I haven't let you." Robin responded kindly, "Well, it's only polite to offer."

It's also polite to accept. More important, it's essential to our emotional health. We need to be nurtured and cared for by others. We need to receive as well as to give.

If you're blessed with significant others who are warm and caring, you already have easy access to nurturing and caregiving. If, like Carole, you're in a situation where significant others are emotionally unavailable or incapable of nurturing, consider going outside those relationships. Following are some strategies and suggestions.

• *Find a support group.* Support groups specialize in mutual acceptance and warmth. If you join a 12-Step group, other members will probably suggest that you choose a sponsor, someone who will be available to you as much as possible to provide caring concern.

• *Adopt a family.* Maybe your birth family isn't particularly nurturing. Or maybe geographical separation has made nurturing impractical or impossible. Why not "adopt" a family member — or a whole family?

I'm not referring here to legal adoption. There are other forms of "adoption." You can choose to connect with a person or group for the express purpose of sharing customs, pleasures, ideas, traditions, and above all, feelings.

Begin by clarifying your own image of the ideal family. This will be a personal vision — one which you can follow as you approach prospective "adoptees" to see if they are willing to join your family. To be real, we need to be direct with others about our desire to "adopt" them. Otherwise we set up a sticky situation where we have expectations of them and they have no idea what we want. This has to do with boundaries — how we are with friends or coworkers is much different from how we are with family. If we expect others to meet our needs without their agreement, we are violating their boundaries — we are using them — and we are bound to end up saddened and disappointed through our own actions.

"Adoption" is far different from finding a friend. It involves discussing and negotiating the roles each of you will play. It requires being open about your needs. For example, you may want a "father" who will celebrate the achievements in your life, an "aunt" who will listen during sad or troubled times without giving advice, an entire "family" you can spend holidays with. Spell out your needs, wants, and hopes as you approach each prospective "family member." The more open you are, the more likely it is that you will find a good fit.

If this idea appeals to you but you're not sure where to start, try imagining your ideal family using characters from movies, books, and TV programs. One of my clients imagined Bill Cosby as her father, Michael Learned as her mother, Michael J. Fox as her brother, and Oprah Winfrey as her sister.

• *Volunteer*. Put yourself in situations where you can feel good about yourself and others. Love and caring are available by the bushelsful from children and elders. Volunteer in clubs and organizations for kids and you'll have more affection than you know what to do with. Nursing homes are begging for friendly visitors or volunteers for "Adopt-a-Grandparent" programs, where your investment of time and openness will be richly rewarded.

The more love and caring you get, the more you can give. The more you give, the more you get. Love doesn't divide; it multiplies.

CHAPTER ELEVEN

COGNITIVE DISTORTION

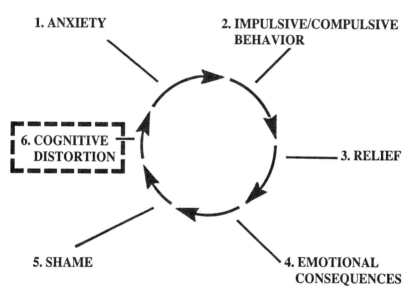

1. ANXIETY

2. IMPULSIVE/COMPULSIVE BEHAVIOR

6. COGNITIVE DISTORTION

3. RELIEF

5. SHAME

4. EMOTIONAL CONSEQUENCES

Cognitive Distortion Defined

"Cognitive distortion" is one of those terms that cries out for definition. "Cognitive" means "having to do with the act of knowing, perceiving and being aware." "Distortion" means "pulled or twisted out of shape, made crooked, misrepresented, falsified." Together these two words describe a thinking process which is warped and twisted. Like the mirrors in a carnival funhouse, which reflect only crooked and false images, cognitive distortion garbles the way we see ourselves and the world.

Like the other phases of the shame-anxiety cycle, cognitive distortion is neither clear-cut nor free-standing from the others. The way we think affects the way we feel and behave. The way we feel affects the way we behave and think. The way we behave affects the way we think and feel. This chapter explores some of the distorted thinking patterns we engage in, examines their relationship to our feelings and behaviors, and considers their contribution to the shame-anxiety cycle.

Forms of Cognitive Distortion

Cognitive distortion comes in many forms. Learning about these can enhance our understanding of this phase of the shame-anxiety cycle.

"Stinking Thinking"

Used by people in Alcoholics Anonymous (A.A.) to describe rigid, grandiose thinking, the term "stinking thinking" applies equally well to the cognitive distortions which are typical of a shame-based identity. "Stinking thinking" applies to the either/or split generated by shame — the all/nothing, black/white, right/wrong, for me/against me thinking patterns that contribute to anxiety and impulsive/compulsive behavior.

The underlying message is almost always based on a distorted perception that what matters to *us* is the most important factor. For example: "I have to get the dishes done right after dinner or I'm just not happy" has the underlying message, "It doesn't matter what my husband's or children's needs are, I'm going to do the dishes!" Or: "You should do the dishes right after dinner. That's how my mother did it," has the underlying message, "I have the right to set the standards around here. I don't care if you're tired from working all day."

Self-centered and rigid, stinking thinking is denial of shame's inherent ability to open our boundaries to others to feel what they feel and perceive the world through their eyes. Ultimately it is a denial of our capacity to feel empathy, compassion, and altruism. Just as our solar system would be out of balance if one of the minor planets suddenly became the center of the universe, so, too, do people get out of balance when they begin to assume a distorted sense of importance. Stinking thinking violates others by turning them into objects to meet our needs or wishes, regardless of their own feelings about the matter.

> "What are they trying to do to me?" sobbed the young mother who had recently heard that her daughter's teacher had charged her with negligence. "I've always tried to be a good mother. I've always taken her to Sunday School!" When I suggested that the teacher was concerned because her daughter didn't have clean clothes to wear to school, or warm clothes to protect her from the winter

weather, the mother became angry. "But what about me?" she insisted. "Do they think I enjoy having old clothes to wear?"

Her stinking thinking — her rigid definition of adequate mothering as one small aspect of caregiving — left her unable to empathize with her daughter's situation. She could only focus on how she felt and thought.

Enid shook her head in confusion. "I simply can't understand where he's coming from!" she said about her husband. "First he tells me he had this affair with my best friend. Then he tells me it's all my fault — that if I hadn't asked her to babysit it never would have happened. He says I don't spend enough time with him, and he's the one who insisted that I go to work to help pay the bills. Then he says if I promise to change he'll take me back — and he's the one who was unfaithful!"

Her husband's self-centeredness not only kept him from being responsible. It also affected her own ability to think clearly.

Negative Self-Talk

Negative self-talk is a continuous, habitual, often unconscious internal dialogue based on distorted expectations of ourselves and our environment. It can become so ingrained that it feels "natural" and we forget there are other ways to think. We sink into a shame swamp of "always, never, have to, must, should." We put ourselves down, call ourselves names, deny our feelings and perceptions, berate ourselves regardless of our achievements. Neither praise nor recognition can penetrate the constant stream of negative self-talk.

When Karen Carpenter collapsed and died of anorexia, we were puzzled to learn how negative and critical she had been of herself and her performances. To the rest of the world, she sang like an angel.

"You are such a goof-up!" went **Leonard's** negative self-talk. "You had a perfectly good job, and what did you do? You threw it away and got yourself in this spot! You should have known better than to trust yourself to make a decent decision. You haven't done anything right yet. Chances are you never will!"

Irrational Thinking

Irrational thinking is repetitive and unthinking. It is driven or activated by our feelings in response to words and personalities. For example, if someone says something we "don't like," or if we "don't like" them, we give ourselves permission to be abusive, controlling, judgmental, critical, explosive. We don't give ourselves time to slow down, consider the facts, and plan our response. We jump to conclusions based on how we feel, instead of on factual information. Irrational thinking is like a short-circuit in the brain.

Our thinking becomes irrational when it leads us to make rules for our lives based on what has happened in our past. This becomes a problem when we try to take a rule which has helped us survive — such as "Watch out, bad things may happen." Rather than being flexible, taking in new information and adjusting our point of view, it's as though we take our life experience and use it as if we were reversing a telescope. We start believing that the rest of the world is identical to our small part of it. We become rigid in our thinking, refusing to accept any new information that doesn't fit with our basic view of life: "Don't bother me with facts, my mind is made up." Ironically, it's seldom our mind that's running the show. It's our feelings. And feelings, like alcohol/other drugs, can leave us incapable of clear, rational thinking.

The bottom line is this: If we believe that everyone in our world is out to get us, that's irrational thinking. If we believe that every unpleasant or unwanted situation we find ourselves in is someone else's fault, that's irrational thinking. If we believe that we must blame or assign fault for every unpleasantness before we can get on with our lives, that's irrational thinking.

Judgmentalism

If we imagine the process of rigid, either/or thinking as a rainbow where one end represents black and the other white, it's easy to see that we're missing a spectrum of beautiful colors. Similarly, judgmentalism splits life into opposite poles of right and wrong, ignoring everything in between. Daily living takes enormous energy because we assume that every situation must be sorted into only two categories, right or wrong.

Pretend that you're a king sitting on a throne. Every day you're called upon to judge whether each situation that occurs in your kingdom is right or wrong. From morning until night, supplicants come before you, asking you to decide on matters like, "Is it right or wrong for me to have toast for breakfast instead of bagels?" "Is it right or wrong to vacuum the floor before the furniture is dusted?" "Is it right or wrong to squeeze the toothpaste in the middle of the tube?" "Is it right or wrong for my boss to ask us to work overtime when she knows it will drive labor costs sky-high?" "Is it right or wrong for the rain to fall today?" Imagine how exhausted you'd be!

This form of cognitive distortion compels us to spend our days unconsciously judging ourselves and the world. "Bagels for breakfast?

You've got to be kidding!" "Anybody with an ounce of sense knows that you dust the furniture first!" "Squeeze the toothpaste in the middle? Are you crazy?" "More overtime! Your boss doesn't know beans about good management." And, "This is awful, but I guess I should have known better than to expect sunshine on a day I planned a picnic."

Judgmentalism is exhausting — physically, emotionally, intellectually, spiritually. It's anxiety-provoking — having to decide about everything is a big responsibility! We fear making a mistake. And when we do, which is inevitable, we consciously or unconsciously label ourselves with a shaming statement: "I am wrong, therefore I am worthless, defective, unlovable."

Self-Fulfilling Prophecies

Another type of cognitive distortion — self-fulfilling prophecy — sets up a negative feedback loop in our heads. Because daily living consumes so much energy, we become exhausted. Because we are exhausted, we perceive life as difficult. Because we perceive life as difficult, that's the way it is. We are caught in a self-fulfilling prophecy.

A self-fulfilling prophecy is an internal prediction that leads to the very event we are predicting. Consider this story:

A man drives up to the country and sees an old gentleman rocking on his front porch. "How are the folks around here?" the man asks. "How were they where you came from?" the gentleman responds. "Really rotten," the man replies. "Not a good neighbor in the bunch. Everybody was out for themselves." "Yup," the old gentleman says, "that's the kind you'll find around here." The man drives away.

As the gentleman sits rocking, another man drives up and asks, "What kind of folks live around here?" Again the gentleman replies: "How were they where you came from?" The man in the car smiles and says, "Great! It was hard to find better people. We sure do wish we'd been able to hang around there, the people were so good." The old gentleman leans forward in his rocker and assures the man, "Yup, that's the kind you'll find around here."

The moral of this story is: We find what we're looking for.

After several years of stress in their marriage — the death of a parent, two children graduating and leaving home, a serious illness for **Evelyn**, a new job for **Leonard** — they were both extremely sensitive to one another's distress signals.

"I can tell the minute I step in the door whether it's going to be safe to talk to Evelyn," Leonard said defensively. "I take one look at her and head for my workbench in the basement."

"It's really bad," Evelyn agreed. "I watch for Leonard to come up the driveway. I can tell from his walk what kind of a mood he's in. Then I get braced for when he comes in the door."

As they comprehended how each of them was preparing "for the worst," they laughed, realizing how frequently they found it.

If we believe we deserve to have bad or don't deserve to have good happen for us, we find even more evidence fulfilling our distorted prophecy that we are being punished, that life is a desperate battle.

"See?" **Roland** said upon learning that I was leaving for a new position. "As soon as you begin to like someone, they just get up and leave. What good does it do? A person is safer not caring!"

Identifying and Changing Cognitive Distortion

Psychologist Constance Avery-Clark has developed a method for identifying irrational thought patterns which create anxiety and contribute to inappropriate behaviors. In her workshops, she teaches people how to reduce anxiety-provoking thinking patterns as a way to stop behavior that violates others. Avery-Clark believes that identifying irrational thinking is the first step toward replacing it with rational thinking.

External events take place. We assess them as "okay" or "not okay." If an event is "okay," we are likely to respond with happiness and satisfaction. The irony of cognitive distortion is that we may still respond with anxiety because we believe that we don't deserve to have good (okay) events happen in our lives. When we believe we deserve the bad, feelings of happiness and satisfaction can actually trigger anxiety: "I know this can't last. With my luck . . . ," followed by a list of awful events we expect to happen. It's as if we think we must pay in pain for any pleasure we experience.

If an external event is "not okay," we experience anxiety that necessitates making a decision. We have three options to choose from:

1. This happened because something outside of me made it happen. Or:
2. This happened because I made it happen. Or:
3. Sometimes these things happen.

If we are trapped in the shame-anxiety cycle, we habitually choose one of the first two options. This triggers uncomfortable emotional consequences: anger, guilt, disappointment, discouragement, rage, depression. We strike out at ourselves or others, justifying or excusing our behavior with the irrational belief that we (or they) deserve to have bad things happen.

Avery-Clark sees irrational thinking as a process of escalating anxiety and "catastrophizing" that goes something like this:

a. Things are not okay.
b. They never go my way and never will.
c. It isn't fair. Why me? I don't like this.
d. I want things to be different, and I want it right now.
e. When things don't go my way, it's terrible, awful, horrible.
f. I feel like I'm out of control and I can't do anything to fix it.

This process feels "natural," but it's actually a learned pattern of cognitive distortion.

If we respond to "not okay" events by blaming others (option 1 above), the next stage of our irrational thinking process goes something like this:

a. It's all their fault. They're trying to get me.
b. How dare they do this to me.
c. Since it's their fault, they'd better fix it.
d. If they're too stupid or uncaring to fix it, the problem will never be solved, so all I can do is . . .
e. Do something to them to show them how much I hurt (strike out physically, verbally, destructively).

If we blame ourselves (option 2, above), the next stage of our irrational thinking process will be similar to the "what-the-hell" syndrome described earlier. ("If the situation can't be fixed right now and just right, then what-the-hell, we might as well quit trying!") The process goes something like this:

a. It's all my fault. I keep screwing myself up.
b. Since it's all my fault, I've got to do something to fix it, but...
c. I'm too stupid to do it right, so all I can do is . . .
d. Take it out on myself (punch a wall, destroy property, push people away physically or emotionally) and then I'll feel better.

Do these descriptions sound familiar? Your Anxiety Log can help you track your thinking and become skilled at recognizing cognitive distortion. (If you haven't started keeping an Anxiety Log, see pages 50-54.) Then you can start learning new, rational thinking patterns to replace the old irrational ones.

Rational thinking is based on acceptance of our limitations to control the world around us. It is self-responsible, self-aware thinking. Because it helps us move away from grandiosity and self-centeredness, we cease to measure the world around us in terms of how we like it. In short, rational thinking moves us into the realm of reality, a world where sometimes things go our way and sometimes they don't.

Rational thinking reduces anxiety, clears the mind, and facilitates effective problem-solving. There will always be problems in life; one of the most common irrational expectations is that happiness means having no problems. Replacing that expectation with the statement "Sometimes these things happen" (option 3, above) is the first step in rational thinking, which goes something like this:

a. Sometimes these things happen. Sometimes they go my way, and sometimes they don't.

b. These are the facts, fair or not. Things are as they are.

c. I'm not going to be able to have it my way all the time.

d. That may not be desirable, but it isn't a disaster.

e. Although I don't feel in control, I have some control over and choice in fixing this and dealing with it.

f. If I spend time blaming myself or others, I'll just waste energy I could be using to solve the problem.

g. This will take time and patience. I will have to slow down.

h. I may not be able to come up with the best solution, but I have a better chance of coming up with a good one if I take time to think about it instead of acting on my emotions.

i. I may not feel good while I'm trying to fix it, but I can live with that.

Complete this process by acknowledging the change you have made and affirming your ability to think rationally. Some self-rewarding statements include:

• It worked. It wasn't easy, but I did better than last time.
• I'm doing better at this all the time.
• I actually got through that without getting uptight.
• That wasn't as hard as I thought.

Self-rewarding may be difficult for you to do. Taking compliments from ourselves is as hard as taking compliments from others, especially if we believe we don't deserve them. Often we hear people minimizing and denying the importance of things they have done to manage their lives

110

more effectively.

> **Norma** blushed when she was asked if she had been able to give herself credit for a week of abstinence from her self-induced bulimic vomiting. "I don't know why I should," she replied. "I should be able to quit that stuff now that I'm out of college." Still believing that she didn't deserve the good, Norma found it impossible to compliment herself on her accomplishment.

Turning Shoulds Into Coulds

Norma illustrates another variation of cognitive distortion, a kind of thinking psychiatrist Karen Horney has labeled "the tyranny of the shoulds." It is a combination of judgmentalism, self-blaming, and negative self-talk that is emotionally and psychologically abusive.

Identifying this form of irrational thinking is fairly simple: Watch for "should" and its variations in your self-talk. Key words include "must," "have to," "gotta," "always," and "never." These words are surface indicators of unconscious cognitive distortion that triggers anxiety and perpetuates the shame-anxiety cycle.

The following exercise demonstrates the impact of negative self-talk.

1. Take a moment to think about the tasks or responsibilities you plan to attend to when you stop reading. Choose one to use in this exercise.

2. Make yourself comfortable, close your eyes, and repeat to yourself, "I have to _____." Fill in the blank with the task you chose a moment ago. For example: "I have to put this book away."

3. Repeat this statement to yourself 15 times. Pay attention to how your body responds.

4. Now substitute the words, "I choose to _____," filling in the blank with the same task. For example: "I choose to put this book away."

5. Repeat this new statement 15 times. Pay attention to how your body responds.

You could probably feel the anxiety rising in your body as you repeated the "I have to" statement. Substituting "I choose to" had an immediate calming effect. You caught a cognitive distortion in the act and calmed yourself through rational thinking — proof that it can be done!

As you become more adept at catching your shoulds, musts, have tos, gottas, alwayses, and nevers, you can start substituting words that reflect your ability to choose your course and be self-regulating. For example, you can change "I have to do the laundry" to "I plan to do the laundry now." Other examples include:

- "I should have them over to dinner" becomes "I want to have them over to dinner."
- "I must meet the deadline" becomes "I can meet the deadline."
- "I have to go now" becomes "I'm leaving now."
- "I always forget to pay my bills on time" becomes "I choose to send my bills out by the first of the month."
- "I never get anything done around here" becomes "Sometimes there's too much to get done in one day."

Turning shoulds into coulds interrupts the shame-anxiety cycle. It accentuates the positive, reminds us that we are capable of making good choices, takes the pressure off, reduces anxiety, and frees our energy for more positive ways of dealing with life.

Using "I Messages"

Just as "I messages" help us to identify and express our feelings, they can also help to interrupt cognitive distortion. Recall that the "I message" has three parts:

1. I feel . . .
2. Because . . . or When . . ., and
3. I'd like . . . .

In this case, substitute "I believe" or "I think" for "I feel." Owning your beliefs and opinions affirms your self-worth. It can also point out times when you are engaging in irrational thinking. For example, you may believe that people should agree with you. If so, say it: "I believe that people should agree with me." It doesn't sound rational because it isn't. But it's out in the open now and you can deal with it. You can challenge your own thinking.

Often we cover up what we're thinking, or we try to manipulate others to agree with us, by using language like, "Don't you think it's about time we balanced the federal budget?" Try owning your belief by saying, "I believe it's about time we balanced the federal budget." This may feel awkward at first, as well as risky, but it is respectful both to you and your listener. Practice it until you start to value your own thoughts and beliefs.

Turning Whys Into Whats and Hows

Another way to identify and change your thinking patterns is by asking yourself a different set of questions. Ordinarily, we ask a lot of "Why?" questions. Too many "whys" in your thinking is almost always a sign of cognitive distortion.

Many 12-Step groups use the term "analysis paralysis" to describe how we keep ourselves from moving on by "thinking about it." "Whys" keep us paralyzed. For a lot of "why" questions, there are no answers. When we persist in our "whys," the underlying message seems to be, "I'm not moving on until I know why!"

As you learn what you really think and believe, as opposed to what you thought were the "right things" to think and believe, you may find it valuable to ask "What?" and "How?" questions. For example: "What makes it so important for everyone to agree with me?" "How am I keeping myself stuck in the same place?" "How could I approach this differently?" Asking yourself a different set of questions is bound to lead to a different set of answers.

Listening To Your Own Wisdom

How often do people come to you for advice about their lives? How often do you give it even when they don't ask for it? Believing that we know the "right way" is another sign of cognitive distortion.

But sometimes we do know the "right way," or we come close. Sometimes our advice is good even if it's free or unasked for. Sometimes the advice we offer to others can help us solve our own problems, even problems we deny or minimize.

Start listening to what you're saying to other people. Give yourself a little credit. If your style is off-putting and full of shoulds, there still may be gems of wisdom in your words. "You should know better than to spend all your money two days after pay day" may contain a valuable admonition. "What you need to do is just keep your mouth shut once in a while instead of blabbing everything you know" sounds rough but may still apply to the situation.

Or maybe you're sympathetic and gentle with others and too hard on yourself. Maybe you've told a friend, "Hey, go easy on yourself. Don't expect yourself to change in a week." Or "I'm really sorry there are so many things going wrong for you just now." Listen to your own wisdom.

Challenging Yourself, Changing Yourself

One of the most effective ways to interrupt cognitive distortion is by giving your brain a workout. Too many of us are indifferent to our intellectual well-being. We maintain our bodies through diet and exercise, take care of our spiritual selves by attending church or synagogue, allow ourselves to express a wide range of feelings, and let the mind take care of itself. Our thinking becomes rigid because we aren't thinking about new ideas.

Challenge yourself intellectually. Exercising your brain is self-affirming and offers many rewards. Learning something new almost always changes you for the better.

Learn a new game. If you feel rusty, start with something on a child's level — and have a child teach you. Most children are patient teachers when it comes to their favorite games.

Play cards, take a class in a subject you're curious about, read a book, join a study club, take a chance by talking about one of your own ideas. Participate in a 12-Step support group, where people talk about their thoughts, feelings, and behaviors while they're learning new ways to live.

PART III:

OVERCOMING BARRIERS TO CHANGE

CHAPTER TWELVE

GRANDIOSITY, PERFECTIONISM, AND THE LOSS OF AUTONOMY

Grandiosity

Up to this point, we have focused on the nature of shame and the shame-anxiety cycle. We have explored ways to free ourselves from the cycle and become self-directing, self-creating individuals guided by our core-self "knowing" of good, truth, morality, virtue, rightness. We have learned how shame can be a positive, transforming power in our lives. If we choose to change, we have at hand many tools and techniques that can help.

This chapter discusses three barriers to change that deplete our energy and divert us from our goal, and offers strategies for overcoming them if we meet them along the way. The first barrier we will consider is grandiosity.

At first glance, grandiosity — an exaggerated, delusional belief that one is powerful, always in control, impressive, magnificent, and always right — seems incompatible with shame. How can someone feel grandiose and at the same time feel bad, worthless, defective, unlovable? It's a paradox. Yet many people trapped in the shame-anxiety cycle are kept there by grandiosity. Here's how their thinking goes:

1. I'm so bad, worthless, defective, and unlovable that I don't deserve the good or do deserve the bad.
2. Others treat me disrespectfully because I'm so bad.
3. Because I'm so bad, I cause others to treat me disrespectfully.

The third statement is the key to understanding the link between grandiosity and shame. It assumes a powerful, impressive ability to make people behave the way they do.

> After **Anna** was badly beaten by her boyfriend, she said with all sincerity, "He wouldn't have done it if I hadn't insisted on having some money for bus fare." When **Sally's** mother was unresponsive to her needs, Sally told herself, "If I didn't ask for food, she wouldn't be so grouchy." When **Paul** learned that his wife had been having an affair, he explained it with, "She wouldn't have done it if I were a better husband."

We've all said things like, "If I hadn't washed my car, it wouldn't have rained." We know that there's really no connection. But there's a hint of grandiosity in such statements, with their implication that we're somehow responsible for external events that are actually beyond our control.

Grandiosity and Shame

The grandiosity-shame connection seems to be rooted in the way shame affects our core self. When we are ashamed, we feel exposed as defective, "less than." This makes us feel helpless and vulnerable, similar to the way we felt as infants when we were totally dependent on others for our emotional and physical survival.

When we were infants, we didn't realize that the decision to care for our needs, or not to care for our needs, lay outside our scope of power. We believed that our crying and body language made our caregivers respond. If they responded by feeding, changing, and holding us, we assumed that was our doing. If they ignored or neglected us, we assumed that was our doing, too.

When shame engulfs us as adults, it takes us back to our infant emotional and psychological state. We believe that we cause the treatment we receive from others and our environment. This is grandiosity. If we are operating out of a shame-based identity, we will return to our infant state so frequently and intensely that grandiosity will color much of our lives.

> **Glenda** struggled to articulate her own sense of grandiosity. "I put myself above people somehow. I put myself in a different category. I tell myself that nobody cares as much as I do." Believing that she had a superior ability to see and care, Glenda also felt burdened with responsibility. "Since I care so much, I guess I'm the one who has to take care of everybody and everything."

Grandiosity and Cognitive Distortion

It's hard to give up the sense of power that goes along with grandiosity, especially if we often experience shame. Grandiosity makes us feel like an imaginary king or queen, the center of attention, universally accepted and admired or feared. It gives us the illusion of being in control of our external world — the people and events that impinge on our lives.

This is the ultimate cognitive distortion, and by believing it we create an impossible task for ourselves. There is simply no way we can control our external world. We can affect it; we can guide, suggest, and plan things we would like to have happen. Our futile attempts to have the world operate our way lead to habitual anxiety.

> "Do you have a problem with control?" **Warren's** therapy group leader asked him. "Not at all," Warren responded. "Just with the people who affect my life!" For Warren, "the people who affect my life" meant everyone whose behavior had some impact on his life, up to and including policymakers in governments at home and abroad whose decisions affected the price of gas or the availability of electrical appliances. The list was endless. Warren was generally angry and frequently exhausted.

Grandiosity diverts our attention from our real task: governing or directing ourselves. When we focus our energies on controlling others, we deny our capacity to change. We convince ourselves that it's easier to change the world than to change ourselves. This is grandiosity — believing that we're worse than the rest of the world put together.

We also deny others the right to effect their own changes. In our grandiosity, we assume that we are the only ones who know how they should be. While we may in fact have some good ideas about things they could do to improve their lives, our rigid, right/wrong thinking and attitude diminish the value of our wisdom.

Finally, we become grandiose in our capacity for martyrdom. We believe we don't deserve the good and take on responsibility that rightly belongs to others: "No, I'll take the night shift even though I've worked all day. You go ahead to your party." We believe we deserve the bad because "only I have the strength to carry this anguish." We shoulder the world's burdens, and we stay trapped in shame.

Letting Go of Grandiosity

Relinquishing our grandiosity and sense of control can be very frightening. It means going against our need for order. It means taking the risk that our needs may not be met. It means struggling against some of our most distorted thinking and facing our own helplessness. As one of my clients said, "It's a terrible disappointment to learn that we alone don't have the power to effect any change we want." Recognizing this is a sure sign of progress.

As **Mike** worked through this phase of his healing, he reported, "I can tell myself that Cathy has a right to dust the furniture after she vacuums the floor, but I still find myself getting uptight. I tell myself that in ten years it won't matter which she does first. I try to put things in perspective. But it's really hard to stop myself from lecturing her about her housecleaning."

Time went by, and Mike reported back again: "I can't believe how free I feel as I get better at letting go of control. I have more energy and enthusiasm for life now that I'm not so anxious about what other people do." He grinned and went on, "Another thing that's really funny is that Cathy has switched to dusting the furniture before she vacuums the floor. She told me that she got so mad at me ordering her around before that she absolutely refused to change, even though it made sense to her, too."

While shame can trigger grandiosity, it can also help us let it go. While part of us "believes" that we can control the world, our sense of shame "knows" how absurd that belief is.

When shame is functioning in this self-correcting capacity, we are often unaware of its workings. We read a want ad for a job that sounds tantalizing and high-paying; for a moment, we fantasize about it, then smile ruefully and go on looking for something that better fits our training and abilities. Or we engage in a free-wheeling political discussion, then smile at ourselves as we end it by saying, "There we go again, solving the problems of the world." We make a suggestion for improving the assembly line, realizing its worth but knowing that it won't fix everything. We want to be as fully accepted as humanly possible, but we understand that not everyone is going to love us.

Shame can help us keep our feet on the ground. It can help us balance our tendencies toward grandiosity. It nudges us toward being our best self without having to be the best.

If you find yourself slipping into grandiosity, an affirmation can be a helpful way to regain your balance. Perhaps one of these sayings can affirm your ability to be self-directing and self-governing:

- "It's okay to feel what I'm feeling. I don't like it, but I can handle it."
- "I can turn this over to my higher power."
- "I can take care of my own needs today."
- "I can take time to calm myself before I act."

"Looking back," **George** says, "I can't believe what it cost me to keep up the fight. I laughed when people told me I was an 'angry young man.' I thought they just didn't understand things the way I did, or they'd be angry, too. I had ulcers, back pains, my marriage broke up, I was perpetually depressed and alcoholic. And all the time, I kept saying, 'When I get this mess straightened out, I won't drink so much.' If I hadn't lost so much, this would be funny. I really did think that I could single-handedly change the world. I thought I was a junior Jesus."

Perfectionism

In our grandiosity, we believe that we can control the world. In our perfectionism, we believe that we can control ourselves to an extreme. We believe that we can become perfect — become Superpeople. Like grandiosity, perfectionism can become a barrier to change because it, too, is based on an illusion: the erroneous belief that people can be perfect.

As Superfamilies populated with Supermom, Superdad, and Superkids, or as Superboss, Superfriend, Superemployee, and on through endless Superselves, we aim to please and we never let go. Yet we still lead lives full of shame.

How Our Role Perceptions
Become Perfectionism

In the past, Superpeople knew where they stood. Superman was primarily a "hard worker" or "dedicated employee." He became known as "Corporate Man," the go-getter who committed to achieving the good things in life through relentless hard work.

Superwoman has also been on the scene for some time. She was the one who got her wash out first on Monday morning, baked the lightest bread, served on the most committees, and had the best-behaved kids in the neighborhood.

Superkids were known as "high achievers." They were expected to follow in their Superparents' footsteps. They were the kids all the other kids hated because parents asked, "Why can't you be like them?"

Superman, Superwoman, and the Superkids are receiving a lot of attention these days. Men and women are moving into new roles — women into the workplace and occupations that were closed in the past; men into new expectations in parenting, negotiating household chores, and relating to others emotionally. Children are being pressured as never before to perform, with childhood seen primarily as a critical preface to achievement of "success."

With this kind of social pressure to achieve, we become more susceptible to perfectionism. Those of us who operate out of shame are especially vulnerable to being swept up in the drive to be Superpeople because of our existing tendency to "do," to push ourselves, to perform. Thus a child who goes into a special computer class may spend extra hours trying to achieve a level of competency that was completely unexpected of a child in the past.

Our expectations are not as simple now. Somehow we have come to accept that we can "have it all" — career, family, social and community involvement (although we often end up feeling as though we've "had it").

As we all move into new roles — for example, women into investment banking, firefighting, and management positions; men into being the nurturing parent instead of simply being the provider, or into more equal participation in household chores; children into preschool instead of a home setting — we are at risk of being triggered into the shame-anxiety cycle. That can happen because change seems to carry with it some degree of anxiety.

If we are people who base our value or self-worth on our performance, we are at further risk. If we have major life changes where we have to learn many new rules at any given time, our vulnerability to shame increases even more. Consider all the new roles that are involved in a life change we all take for granted, such as a new job or promotion. The job description is different; we may need to learn a lot of new skills; we relate to people differently — we may now be an "equal" and not a "subordinate," or a "supervisor" of people who were our "friends;" we may qualify for new "perks" and become a company "stockholder;" we may be an "exempt employee," expected to work longer hours without overtime pay, which in turn affects our relationship with our spouse as we become a more "dedicated employee," and on and on. There are many new ways to "be," many new roles in which to pressure ourselves to perform at a high level.

Over and over, I see people who have sustained a tremendous number of major life changes over the past year or two or three, such as graduating from college, moving to a new city, taking a new job, breaking up a romantic relationship, perhaps experiencing a death or a serious illness in their family. They are depressed, discouraged, and ashamed, saying, "I've always been able to handle things before. There must be something really wrong with me for me to feel this bad!" They push themselves even deeper into the shame swamp, saying, "Other people handle these things. What's wrong with me?" For the most part, they have tumbled head-first into perfectionism, the expectation that despite life changes they will continue to perform at a high level in every role or aspect of their lives.

The Compulsion to Measure Ourselves

Perfectionists judge themselves and others by the small details of their lives.

Lance told how he lay awake at night, going over and over the presentation he had made at the board meeting that day: "Maybe I just didn't say it right. If I knew the right words then I'd be okay." **Jeanie** agonized over the choice of a restaurant to entertain her mother-in-law: "I don't want her to think I'm extravagant, but I don't want her to think I didn't want to take her someplace nice." **Karen** reviewed her performance on a math test: "I should have been able to get that last problem. It's so stupid to miss it." She ignored the reality that she had correctly completed all the other problems on the test.

When we slip into perfectionism, we evaluate our "doing" at the expense of our "being." Have we achieved more this week than last? Have we spent "quality time" with our children lately? When was the last time the garage was cleaned? We measure and measure until the act of measuring becomes as unconscious and unthinking as an inchworm's progress along a branch. We can no longer tell if we are measuring mountains or molehills. We judge ourselves as critically on our smallest failings as we do on our largest. The more we measure, the more anxious we become.

The compulsion to measure ourselves is a real Superproblem. It operates on three levels. First, we measure ourselves against illusion. Second, we measure ourselves against people who excel. And third, we measure ourselves in every role and aspect of our lives.

Measuring Ourselves Against Illusion

Gordon justified his harsh discipline of his children by saying, "It worked for my dad!" **Kelly** explained, "When I talk to other mothers who have children the same age as my nine-month-old daughter, and I find out that she isn't doing the same things they are, I feel like I have to justify her to them." **Marcie** puffed around the track at the gym, thinking, "If Joannie runs three hours a week and looks as fit as she does, I'm going to run four hours!"

All three are measuring themselves against illusions: an illusion of successful parenting, an illusion of ideal infant development, an illusion of fitting one's body to someone else's standards.

Many of us measure ourselves against the illusion of Family. Most of us still define Family as a mother, father, and children who live in the same household, with mother not employed outside the home. In our minds, Family means the Cleavers of "Leave it to Beaver." The very act of judging ourselves by these unrealistic standards reveals that we're caught in the shame-anxiety cycle.

We know that nearly two out of every three women work outside the home. We know that many households are headed by single parents or are blended families. We know that more unmarried singles are living together. Yet we persist in our illusion of Family. We leave no room to accept ourselves as single heads of households, step-parents, dual-career families, couples deferring parenthood, same-sex couples, or any of the diverse other forms a family today can take. We continue to measure ourselves against the illusion of Family.

This puts tremendous pressure on us to be SuperFamily members. Because this goal is impossible to achieve, we feel defective, "less than," and ashamed.

"If I were a better grandfather," **Dick** said, "I could watch my grandkids more to help out my daughter." This from a man who was on the road as a salesman during the week, and already babysat his grandsons almost every weekend.

Measuring Ourselves
Against People Who Excel

Here is where we really do a number on ourselves. First we measure ourselves against a person who is truly unique — a Mother Teresa, Lee Iacocca, Michael Jordan, or Oprah Winfrey. Then, by presuming the necessity of measuring ourselves against someone of superior abilities, we actually deprive ourselves of a legitimate role model, a person we can look up to and learn from.

A Mother Teresa is a human phenomenon that occurs very rarely. She is a marvelous example of how humans can function at a high level of shame-defeating love. But if we measure ourselves against her, we can only come out wanting. We are bound to feel "less than" Mother Teresa. We shame ourselves by not accepting our own abilities, our own ideal of what we can be.

We can use this tendency to measure ourselves against the greatest as a way to catch our own Superperson leanings. Because we believe that we have to be perfect, we assume that our heroes and heroines are. We take it for granted that they excel in every part of their lives. And this makes us feel even worse and more flawed.

Life is not an either/or situation. There is room in the world for much excellence, in varying forms and degrees. More importantly, there is room in the world for us regardless of how we "do." It's enough simply to "be."

When we measure ourselves against other people, we are being disrespectful of ourselves. We are denying our own reality.

The last of six children, **Lucia** stood in the footprints of brothers and sisters who had excelled in a wide variety of activities — leads in plays, awards in musical competitions, scholastic excellence, athletics. "I hate being a little Brooking!" she said. "I'm not as good at anything as any of them!" Despite her own abilities, she stopped herself from trying because she measured herself against her siblings.

Measuring Ourselves in Everything We Do

As we stretch for perfection, we feel compelled to be the best in everything we do, every role we play, every aspect of our lives. Reaching a high level of achievement in one area isn't good enough for us. We measure ourselves by what we have done, and what we may have left undone.

We compare unrelated areas of our lives against each other. Superkids measure their self-worth by their grades. Superwomen measure their lovability or worth by the size of their paychecks. Predictably, measuring ourselves so irrationally leads to feelings of anxiety. We are constantly on the lookout for more ways to validate our worth and guard against exposure or defectiveness. We focus so intensely on our inadequacies that we do the very thing we fear: We expose ourselves and point at our inadequacies to prove our defectiveness.

We also compare the many roles we play against one another. In a typical day, we may be a parent, a friend, a spouse, a lover, an employee, a customer, a member of the volleyball team, a son or daughter, a colleague or coworker. We expect ourselves to measure up in every role or risk exposure, possibly abandonment.

In some cases the risk of rejection may be real, since there are people who are willing to accept us only if we perform to meet their standards. That is a different situation than meeting self-imposed standards out of an unrealistic fear of abandonment. As you gain in your ability to assess your own perfectionism, you will also gain in your ability to realize when you are having control or power struggles with others — and make more effective decisions about them.

It's important to note that all high achievers are not Superpeople. There is a marked difference between those who accomplish a lot because they are full of energy, and those who accomplish a lot because they are on the Superperson track. The former almost always operate out of a zest and enthusiasm for life. Hans Selye, the father of stress studies, calls them "race horses." They experience few negative consequences because their energy is genuine, not based on the anxiety drive, and their being is in balance.

In contrast, Superpeople plod through life feeling like martyrs, doing "what we have to do" because "we have to do it or it won't get done." Our rallying cry is, "Somebody has to do it!" Denial keeps us from recognizing our underlying efforts to control our situation so "we won't feel anxious." We insist that "we want others to help," and on those rare occasions when we delegate some of our responsibilities, we complain "I tried to get some help but they just didn't do it right." (It's fairly easy to guess whose version of "right" we mean.) We end up feeling isolated and alienated.

When **Beth and Elliott** married, they talked a lot about how their family was going to be "different." Both of them had career plans, both of them wanted children, both of them were committed to shared parenting. Nevertheless, when their first child arrived, friction between the two of them seemed to be part of the package.

"Hold her head up, Elliott, or she might get hurt!" "It's obvious you haven't diapered a baby before." "Elliott, don't you know the snaps on the pajamas go down the back?" Smarting from the stream of criticism, Elliott gradually withdrew from childcare. Meanwhile Beth became increasingly resentful as she found herself carrying "more of the load." When their resentments exploded one night in a fierce argument, they realized how unhappy they were.

As they talked the problem out, Beth realized how she had taken over the childcare as a way to deal with her unexpected feelings that she wasn't a good mother if she wasn't at home with her daughter all the time. Elliott, on the other hand, was feeling inadequate, defective as a father, because he wasn't "on top of the daddy job description."

The Need for External Affirmation

Superpeople focus on external affirmations of worth, and there seem to be big payoffs if we play the part well. We are rewarded with admiration: "I don't know how you manage to get everything done, and so well!" We receive positive reinforcement in the form of bigger paychecks and promotions. We gain power within our relationships.

We also get to do the jobs that could have been done by others, robbing them of the satisfaction of carrying out their own responsibilities. And we continue to deny our own needs. Our so-called "payoffs" keep us trapped in our compulsion to prove ourselves by doing.

To her credit, **Beth** was able to recognize how "taking over" the childcare had a payoff for her: By "carrying more of the load," she was able to relieve her own anxiety about her mothering role. In the process, she was robbing Elliott of the satisfaction he felt in his involvement with their daughter.

Beth denied her own need for help with childcare, pushing herself to find the extra time, doing without sleep at times.

"Since our argument," she told me, "I've found another payoff that is kind of weird. When the women sit around the office complaining about their husbands, I feel more a part of the group when I complain, too. They really don't want to hear about how wonderful Elliott is about getting up for the 2 a.m. feeding."

Private vs. Public Life

One of the crazy-making aspects of growing up in a Superfamily is that private life (what really goes on) is so often different from public life (what other people see).

David gave Martha a look of immense gratitude as he said, "You're the first person who ever understood what it was like to have a mother who 'loved' me so much. Growing up with her was like being smothered in cotton candy. It was sweet, but it still smothered me. Everyone else told me how lucky I was to have such a loving mother."

David's Supermother "loved" him into compliance with her rigid standards. He grew up believing he was a rotten son for feeling angry at his "loving" mother.

Although both **Ardis** and her husband earned incomes, he allowed her to make no decisions about how family money was spent. When I challenged her for defending him, she angrily said, "But everybody thinks he's wonderful. At the office party, three — THREE — of his coworkers came to me to tell me how lucky I am to be married to such a nice guy."

The crazy-making comes from all the admiration generated by those who see only the public Superperformance, not the private damage being done. People on the outside see the Scoutmaster who is beloved by all the kids he comes into contact with; they don't see how he deprives his own children by spending all his time on troop business.

Perfectionism and Relationships

Perfectionism leaves little room for genuine relationships. On the surface, it may look as though people are important; as the workaholic parent says, "I'm doing it so the kids can have the best." The Scoutmaster may genuinely enjoy children. However, these relationships are almost always superficial and manageable because they allow us to fit our behaviors to the roles we are in. The Scoutmaster is trained in "how to be" with his troop; Ardis's husband is trained in "how to be" a manager. Both can rely on the expectations that accompany their roles.

"My staff respects me," **Arnie** stated vigorously. "They call me Mr. Merrill. When I tell them what's expected, they just do it and don't give me any backtalk. It's different at home. Both the boys are getting mouthy. Right now, they're complaining they ought to get an allowance. When I was their age, I was out earning money! Then Ardis jumps in to tell them to be quiet and not bother me.

127

The first thing you know, we've got another fight on our hands. Of course I'd rather spend time with the people from the office. They appreciate me!"

In contrast, genuine personal relationships tend to be messy. There aren't many rules for "how to be." If there is a rule at all, it's probably this: "Be real. Be genuine. Be you." This can be very frightening for the shame-based person. We fear being exposed as unlovable, defective, "less than." Every time we turn around, every time we take part in the relationship, we face a new and slightly different situation because each of us is growing and changing.

Overcoming Perfectionism

Perfectionism can be a refuge. Inside, we're anxious and hurting; to the rest of the world, we're Superperson! It can be very difficult to let go and just "be," especially if we are operating out of a shame-based identity. We turn to "doing," covering up our "being" with some kind of activity. We count the pieces of mail ready to leave the office, or look at the bottom line of today's sales. Then we say to ourselves, "Wow, look what I did today! That means I'm okay."

On the other hand, if we choose to sit with a sick child or spend time with a friend in need, we may think to ourselves, "I haven't accomplished a thing all day." Our shame-anxiety leads us to overvalue our doing and undervalue our being. The most effective way to overcome perfectionism is by treating it like a cognitive distortion. Superpeople are full of shoulds, have to's, gottas, and musts; see pages 111-112 for ways to start turning shoulds into coulds.

"I've been so much better this week," **Donna** beamed. "I've been able to sleep, and I think I've enjoyed the kids more than I have for months." What had made such a difference? Donna herself.

"Usually when I get home from work or the classes I teach," she said, "the first thing I do is fix dinner. By the time that's done I'm ready to collapse, so I really like to sit down and watch a TV show or maybe play a game with the kids. Ordinarily I'd be ragging myself all the time — 'You'd better get the dishes done . . . Throw in some laundry . . . Clean up a little.'

"Last week I decided a few dirty dishes weren't going to tarnish my reputation too badly. I'd just take time to do something I enjoyed. And you know what — I really did enjoy it! I can't believe something so simple could make such a difference."

It's not easy to give up being a Superperson. But, as psychologist Edith Gomberg says, "There is a middle ground: doing the best you can, accepting one's own limits, doing for others without paying too heavy a price, doing for oneself without abandoning another's needs."

The Loss of Autonomy

Autonomy can be defined as the ability to be self-governing and independent, to act upon our core-self "knowing" of how we can be. From observing people at times of change, I have concluded that whenever our sense of autonomy is threatened or violated, we are at risk of feeling shame.

Times of change in our life are times when we can expect to feel vulnerable. These might include the aging process, retirement, going from elementary school to junior high, having a child, the death of a family member, facing a major illness. It would be impossible to list them all. The point to keep in mind is that whenever you are dealing with major life changes, they carry with them the risk of feeling shame. And it doesn't seem to matter whether these changes are desirable or undesirable.

Shame and Desirable Life Change

It's confusing to feel shame in the midst of a happy event or life change. Our inability to name what is happening to us contributes to our confusion. It doesn't make sense to feel exposed and ashamed simply because we're retiring or starting a new school.

What happens is that we're forced by the life change to take on a new role — retiree, seventh grader. While formerly we operated autonomously in the role we knew — employee, sixth grader — the rules have suddenly changed. We are cast on the stage of life without having learned our lines. We feel shame because we can no longer act as autonomously as we did in our former role.

If we are operating out of a shame-based identity, we are at risk of feeling the same old feelings even more intensely because of the additional pressures from the life change. The Chinese symbol for crisis also means opportunity, but in this case the opposite is equally true: Opportunity carries within it the seeds of crisis. Being aware of this can help you avoid the pitfalls of your shame-based past. You may be able to interrupt or head off some of your old coping mechanisms and stay out of the shame-anxiety cycle.

When **Lorraine** was named Employee of the Month, she found herself feeling jittery, restless, unable to sleep. She dreaded the official presentation, knowing all eyes would be on her and fearing what people might be thinking.

As soon as she became aware of her increased anxiety, she began a conscious program to help herself get back into balance. She asked a friend to go to coffee with her to talk about her anxiety, and she nurtured herself in other ways — warm baths, a little extra time at her daily meditations, listening to her favorite albums. By the day of the presentation she was able to say, "I don't like the way I've been feeling. I'm angry that the old habits kicked back in because something good has happened to me, but at least I'm going to be able to walk up on stage knowing that I've improved. A year ago I would have made up an excuse to miss the presentation completely."

Shame and Undesirable Life Change

When a life change is unwanted or undesirable, our sense of autonomy is even more threatened. Frequently, for example, loss of employment is seen as an embarrassment. With our identity tied to our occupation, we see ourselves as "less than" if we aren't working. We are more vulnerable to life's problems when we are unemployed. Unsure how to introduce ourselves to strangers, we stammer and don't know what to say.

"It was bad enough when he got laid off from his regular job," **Lucille** said of her husband. "It didn't matter that his whole department was laid off. He moped around and was sure he'd never get another job. It was really terrible when the temporary job he found ended, too. Now he's so ashamed that he won't even leave the house. How can he find a job that way?"

Her husband's sense of autonomy was threatened. His ability to take care of himself and his family had been compromised. He was paralyzed by anxiety and shame.

We may find ourselves avoiding friends or family who have suffered some kind of undesirable life change — the loss of a job, a divorce, the death of a loved one. The assault on their autonomy, and their resulting shame, can invade our boundaries and trigger our own anxiety. We may not even be aware that this is happening. All we know is that we're uncomfortable.

Aging and Illness

Aging and illness are threats to our autonomy. They slow us down and make us more dependent on others to meet our needs. We are vulnerable to their refusal to help; we feel exposed and helpless.

As we talked about anger, **Ruby** acknowledged that she had been quite angry recently. When asked to share what had happened, she talked in a quiet voice about the incident.

Recently Ruby had given up driving because cataracts were impairing her vision. She lives in a small town where she is forced to rely on friends and family for transportation. One day she waited outside her apartment building for a ride to a meeting. Her driver was 45 minutes late. As she waited, she became more and more anxious, then angry, thinking, "Am I really that unimportant? Does she really think that little of me that she wouldn't come to get me? Am I really that terrible to be with that she can't follow through on her promises?" Ruby felt that "the whole world" could see how desperately she wanted that ride — and how defective she must be to be "unable to take care of myself." She felt exposed and ashamed.

Coping with the Loss of Autonomy

Like Ruby, we may feel anger and shame when we are "unable to take care of ourselves". We may feel exposed to the world, embarrassed to be "less than" we have been in the past. We can be pulled into the shame-anxiety cycle regardless of how accomplished or productive we have been in the past. This is so unexpected, based on our past functioning, that when it happens we feel "crazy" because it hasn't happened before.

If we have operated out of shame-based beliefs in the past and have been progressing in our recovery, we can be extremely distressed when we find ourselves back in the shame-anxiety swamp. It feels as though "I'm going back to that again, and I don't ever want life to feel that grim and awful anymore."

If we are aware that loss of autonomy can quickly tug us into the shame-anxiety cycle, we are forewarned that what's happening to us is typical. We can develop a plan more quickly to diminish the intensity of the reaction. We can't avoid it because our humanness makes us vulnerable to the shame response in such situations.

Dr. Elisabeth Kübler-Ross's genius lay in her ability to see the pattern of human response to loss. We go through the stages of denial, bargaining, anger, depression, and acceptance whenever we deal with loss. When we know that what's happening to us or others is part of a predictable process of coming to grips with loss of autonomy, and it can help us cope more effectively.

The Anxiety Log can be an effective way to intervene when we are threatened with loss of autonomy. It can help us to identify our feelings, thoughts, and behaviors in a way that validates them. How we feel is how we feel; we don't have to justify our feelings. We can see if our behaviors are interfering with our ability to reach out for support. For information on how to start and keep an Anxiety Log, see pages 50-54.

In many communities, support groups are available that deal with conditions of aging, chronic pain, illness, and loss. Such groups can help serve as a safety valve for members to ventilate frustrations and other feelings and learn new coping strategies.

CHAPTER THIRTEEN

ROADBLOCKS TO CHANGE

The Role of Anticipation

Whenever we set off on a new adventure, we have a mental image of how it's going to be. We may expect this to be the time when everything comes together — or we may imagine that "with our luck" it will be just one more occasion when it rains on our parade.

Anticipation plays an important role in determining outcome. Now that you've learned about shame and how it affects your life, you have probably formed some expectations or plans for your future. You may be committed to change. Or you may feel shaken by what you've learned and doubt your ability to free yourself from the shame-anxiety cycle.

In my work with my clients, I have discovered eleven common road-blocks to change. You may meet some, all, or none of them on your personal path. Knowing about them in advance may lessen your anxiety. Here, too, your anticipation will influence your progress. If you see each roadblock as an insurmountable barricade, then change will be more difficult for you. Imagine instead that each is an opportunity to climb a little higher and get a better view of where you want to go.

Fear of the New

In *Man and His Symbols*, Carl Jung points out the "existence among primitive peoples of what anthropologists call 'misoneism,' a deep and superstitious fear of novelty." He goes on to explain that primitive peoples aren't the only ones who experience this "fear of the new." It also occurs in those of us who consider ourselves "civilized."

The fear of the new is buried in our unconscious. We may see ourselves as flexible, adaptable, and challenged by new situations, and this may be true on one level. At a deeper level, however, we may be denying the stress that flexibility and adaptability impose on our physical, emotional, intellectual, and spiritual selves. Stress happens regardless of whether a new situation is desirable or undesirable for us. Both eustress (stress that results from something we consider "good") and distress (which results from something we judge to be "bad") require the same amount of adaptation on our part.

Stress can be particularly acute if we're pressuring or forcing ourselves to make a change that triggers a strong "fear of the new" response. If we operate out of a shame-based identity, we may compound our stress by blaming ourselves or others for our fear. The 12-Step groups' saying, "Easy Does It," reminds us to slow down and give ourselves time to make the change, adapt to it, and develop confidence in our ability to maintain it over time.

There's a simple way to check up on your own "fear of the new" response. Just ask yourself, "What am I afraid of today?" Consider the question at different times throughout the day: in the shower, walking from the parking lot to the office, waiting for the spin cycle on the washing machine. Respond as honestly as you can, and log your responses if possible. You'll learn more about your "fear of the new" and deal more effectively with change.

> **Jeff** decided to informally test this question on his friends at their favorite Friday-night hangout. Instead of greeting them with "Hi, what's new with you lately?" he asked, "What are you afraid of lately?" On Monday he told me how authentically his friends had responded. "One said he was afraid that the valves were going out on his truck," Jeff reported. "Another told me he was worried about how things were going between him and his wife."

The Rubber Yardstick

Some self-evaluation is essential to personal growth. Too much becomes a poison that stunts us and can lead to defeat, resignation, helplessness and hopelessness, leaving us disengaged and withdrawn. Afraid to try because we can't measure up to our own impossibly high standards, we stop before we begin. Swamped by shame, we are caught in a downward spiral of feeling exposed, defective, unlovable, helpless to change because we can never be perfect enough.

The use of the "rubber yardstick" is an indicator of excessive perfectionism. Let's say that you set a goal for yourself — perhaps a new car, a larger home, a promotion at work, good grades, or something else you can achieve or "earn." You achieve your goal, expecting to feel satisfied and happy, but then you pull out your "rubber yardstick" and tell yourself, "No, that really isn't quite good enough. I'll get a better car . . . redecorate my home . . . earn $5,000 more a year . . . go for a 4.0 average. Then I'll feel better." You attain your new goal and stretch your "yardstick" even more.

Another example of a rubber yardstick is the double standard. We set one standard for others that is reasonable or even permissive, then set another for ourselves that is unrealistic and rigid. We justify it with thinking like, "It's okay that they don't achieve a great deal; they have the right to decide what they will do. But I know what I should be doing and I'm determined to give it my best shot." Even our best shot isn't acceptable because of a niggling suspicion that "if I had only tried harder, I could have done better."

Self-affirmation can help you throw away your "rubber yardstick" and retire your double standards. Find a small plaque with a message of personal worth and put it someplace where you can see it several times a day. Or try whispering a self-rewarding thought to yourself.

Roy found a poster that proclaimed, "I am one of God's children." He hung it on his bedroom wall so it was the first thing he saw in the morning, the last at night. Whenever he became anxious, he repeated the affirmation to himself to clear his mind. "At first, when I would say to myself, 'I am one of God's children,' I didn't believe it," he explained. "Part of me even scoffed, 'Yeah, sure!' But I would just repeat it — and now I've really begun to believe it.

"Don't get discouraged," he told other group members. "It's worth the effort."

Feelings of Emptiness

Often the shame-anxiety drive pushes us to run, run, run from one activity to another, work long hours, do anything just to keep busy. This hyperactivity seems to fulfill two purposes: It provides some relief from anxiety, even if the cost (exhaustion, physical illness, emotional distress) is high. And it masks feelings of emptiness.

Feelings of emptiness may have their source in the shame-anxiety cycle. The belief that one is defective, unlovable, unworthy, undeserving of the good, and deserving of the bad can lead to almost unbearable hopelessness. In an attempt to control or diminish our pain, we may numb our feelings or disconnect them from our bodies and emotions. The result is a "zero state" of existence, the sense that we might literally cease to exist.

It is very difficult to deal with these feelings by oneself when they are extremely intense. Sometimes psychotherapy is necessary to break the shame-hopelessness-emptiness cycle. Support groups can help, too, especially those where new members are matched with sponsors who have "been there" and are willing to share their experiences. For many people, the answer lies in making a spiritual connection. Here you have several choices: joining a church; joining a 12-Step group that emphasizes turning one's life over to a higher power, personal meditation and prayer.

If you have been a "runner," you are probably using a lot of denial to help cover your feelings of emptiness. Following are some questions you might ask yourself to start breaking through your denial.

- "When I have quiet time, do I find myself feeling bored?"
  Clients have told me, "I get bored very easily." I have come to realize that this comment is often a clue to a terrifying level of anxiety that carries with it a sense of impending disintegration or doom. I have no idea how the word "bored" gets attached to that sensation, but I have observed that phenomenon so frequently that it doesn't seem coincidental.

- "Do I find myself overscheduling my life to avoid quiet times?"
  This can happen for other reasons, too, but it often is a signal that we want to ignore our emptiness.

- "Do I hang out with people who are hurtful and exploitive?"
  If you do, it may be for one or more of these reasons: First, the people you hang out with are full of pain, too, so it feels as if you have some common ground; second, you are so afraid to be alone that you'll settle for someone — anyone — no matter how abusive; third, just as a child would rather be spanked than receive no attention at all, you'll settle for abuse in order to have some sense of contact with others.

- "Do I sometimes find myself striking out verbally or physically for 'no reason at all'?"
  Striking out at others is generally an effort to dump our own pain. This is almost always accompanied by some kind of thinking that justifies our behavior.

- "Do people tell me that I 'space out' a lot?"
  You may not be aware of "numbing out" unless other people comment on it, because this can easily be an unconscious way of dealing with the feelings of emptiness.

The exercise on pages 98-99 can be a good starting point for change. It is crucial to begin gradually. The sense of connectedness to others is one of the most important ways to begin filling the empty hole — and genuine connection simply cannot be rushed.

"It Feels Natural"

Have you ever had a lumpy mattress that you vowed to replace as soon as you could afford it? Every time you crawled into bed, you complained and looked forward to the day when you'd be able to sleep on a new and better mattress.

Nevertheless, you'd come home from an extended trip (with excellent beds) and roll back into your own bed saying, "Boy, it feels good to be home!"

We all have the tendency to return to the familiar. The familiar is known, comfortable, non-threatening. It feels natural to us.

As you work on changing your life, you may find it tempting to return to the familiar — your old ways of being. This doesn't mean you have failed. It may actually mean that you have been working so hard you could use a break, and this is one way to take one. Perhaps you have been pushing yourself too hard to get it right, RIGHT NOW! Give yourself a "feeling break." This may help you become aware of pressures within yourself or your environment to which you are responding with a flight back to the familiar.

Return to your Anxiety Log if you haven't been using it. Or re-read the past several weeks' worth of your log, looking for patterns or signs. You may have been doing so well that you unwittingly put aside tools that have been keeping you on an even keel, believing you don't need them anymore.

The Time Warp Syndrome

Time may fly when you're having fun, but our perceptions of time can become extremely warped when we've been living in the flywheel of the shame-anxiety cycle. As you struggle to move out of your habitual ways of thinking, feeling, and believing, the time-warp syndrome may be a factor in blocking change.

A time warp is rather like Alice walking through the looking glass. It's like being in another dimension, where your perceptions are totally unlike the perceptions of those around you.

> **Lance** stormed into the soup and sandwich shop he operated. "Where is that invoice I needed to wrap up the books for this month?" he demanded angrily. "Didn't you call the purveyor like I asked you to?"
>
> "He'll have it here later this afternoon, when he makes the delivery," the manager replied defensively.
>
> "What in hell is taking him so long?" Lance wanted to know.
>
> Puzzled, the manager said, "But...you didn't ask me to call him until 11:00 this morning. You said then that this afternoon would be soon enough."
>
> In a rage, Lance stormed out — only to return later, apologizing sheepishly for his behavior. He had "lost track of time" and didn't realize that such a brief period if time had elapsed.

Especially for people who have seen time as an enemy, who have been running in place or have seen each day as another endurance contest, the time warp can be defeating simply because they have no sense of how much time has elapsed since they last checked. This distortion can make change seem like an illusion — not coming quickly enough to ease their pain, or whirling away so quickly that there seems to be none left for using the tools of change.

Take it one day at a time. If that seems too much, try one hour, one minute, even one impulse at a time. Make lists and check off your accomplishments for a graphic record of the changes you're making.

The Hope and Fear Two-Step

Any time we make a significant change in our lives, we are subject to the hope and fear two-step. We are filled with hope at the prospect of change; we fear what will happen if we fail (or succeed).

> "I know I don't want to go on like this anymore," **Barry** said. "And I believe I can change. But what if my wife doesn't like me after I change? I can't risk it!"

We are inspired by the hope of healing, and paralyzed by the fear of healing. As another client told me, "I don't want to live in anger anymore. But if I give up my anger, how will I ever have the energy to do what I need to do?"

We know that life can be better. Our knowing may be offset by the fear that our old shame-based belief — that we don't deserve good and do deserve bad — may actually be true.

Our feelings swing back and forth because we have unrealistic expectations of how life will be when we have changed. We want to be "happy," then define "happiness" as the absence of everything we're accustomed to. We think it means that we won't have problems, won't have fears and anxiety, won't have conflict with people we care about, won't have stress in our lives. We promise to stop doing old behaviors: "I won't be angry," "I won't spend too much money," "I won't yell at the kids." We earnestly hope we will stick to our vows. Then the first time we get angry, spend over the budget, or yell at our children, we fear that all our efforts will fail.

If you find yourself caught in this up-and-down, back-and-forth, hope and fear two-step, try changing your focus. On a sheet of paper, make two columns — one for the "pros," the reasons for change, and one for the "cons," the reasons against change. Putting your hopes and fears down in black and white will help define the reality of change for you.

Accentuate the positive. Give yourself credit for reducing the number of times you have fallen into an old impulsive-compulsive behavior. Watch a comedy; read a humorous book.

"It's Too Late to Change"

Once there were three friends, all of whom were facing decisions about their marriages. As they sat drinking coffee together, 48-year-old Adelle mentioned that she was feeling as if she needed to make a decision "before it's too late." Nodding in agreement, 37-year-old Barb said, "That's what I've been thinking." Then 26-year-old Carin burst into laughter and said, "Me, too! Which one of us do you think is 'too late'?"

"Too late" is a state of mind. It doesn't matter how old or young you are or how long you've been trapped in the shame-anxiety cycle. Having made the decision to change, the best time to start is now. You can't change the past; you can't control the future. But today, right now, is in your hands.

You've picked up this book and read this far. Let's build on that desire to change. Change doesn't have to be big to be significant. For example, some people may lay down this book and say something like, "Well, back to work," or "Now I'd better do something practical." Why not resolve to do something different this time? Choose one of the simplest or smallest tools for change, then say aloud, "Now I am going to _____." Fill in the blank with "say a small prayer," "go for a walk before I start working," write down what I'm feeling right now" — you get the idea! If you're the sort of person who procrastinates, perhaps you will opt to complete the monthly report, take care of the shopping, put this book in its proper place. The point is not necessarily to do something big, but to do something now — and to choose something different than you ordinarily would.

When people tell me, "It's too late to change," I say, "Let me tell you about my mother-in-law." She was 56 years old when I met her, a woman of fairly rigid beliefs about how life should and shouldn't be. She had never held an office in the club she had belonged to all her married life because she was embarrassed to speak up in public. She was dependent on her family for transportation because she had "forgotten how to drive." She was unable to show affection through hugs or kisses. Her children had never heard her say that she loved them.

This glorious woman is now 95. She speaks before her church members and at the Senior Citizen's Center. She gave up driving a year ago because her vision became impaired. She has come to believe in her worthiness to give and receive love; she walks up to us with her arms held out for a hug, she can tell us that she loves us. Most wonderful of all, she can accept the love we give to her.

Her life taught me that we can overcome our feelings of shyness, embarrassment, and dependence. When we risk opening our lives and making genuine connections to others, we, too, can change. It's never too late.

Loyalty to Family

According to family therapist Carl Whitaker, we can't overestimate the strength of our loyalty to the "idea of family." I further believe that we can't overestimate the strength of our loyalty to our family of origin. Nor can we overestimate the power of family pressure to stay the same and keep playing the same old roles.

If you put these three together, they are formidable indeed. The "idea of family" acknowledges our deep need for connection with others. Our family of origin is usually where we make our first connections. These are also our most durable connections: No matter how old we are, we want our parents and siblings to accept and care for us.

Our family needs us as much as we need them. Over and over, I've seen situations where individuals have started to change, and their families have done everything they could to keep them from changing. Sometimes this has to do with the fear of spilling "family secrets." Other times it's because the family's precarious balance depends on everyone staying the same. And oftentimes it's because change in one family member may require change on everyone's part. The result is resistance and fear.

Remember that we can't change anyone else. We can only change ourselves. The paradox here is that once we change, others will change in response. When Mike let go of his need to control his wife's vacuuming, Cathy let go of her need to resist his controlling. When an alcoholic stops drinking, the other family members' controlling behavior becomes more obvious, as does the need to change their behavior.

A change in one family member can generate change in the rest of the family. The bottom line is: Change begins with the individual.

Mindy's story is a dramatic example of how this works.

When **Mindy** first came to see me, she was very anxious, bursting into tears "without any reason." She was concerned about her parenting abilities; her two small children were becoming belligerent and difficult to manage. She was shy, almost to the point of being agoraphobic, and she clung to her home, fearful to go out unless accompanied by her husband. The adult child of an alcoholic, she was the one everyone in her family of origin called when trouble developed, and she would speed to the rescue. Her husband, also an adult child of an alcoholic, was estranged from most of his family, seeing them only occasionally. He was given to angry, controlling outbursts which Mindy feared, trembling in dread that this would be the time he finally left her.

During her therapy, Mindy worked on becoming more assertive with her husband and sons. She gradually set limits on when she was willing to be available to help her family and what she would do for them. She began building interpersonal relationships. She practiced her skills with her sons, who were young enough to be accepting and uncritical; she practiced them with strangers at the bus stop, with sales clerks, and finally with friends, then family. She struggled with her belief that she didn't deserve the good as she learned to nurture herself, tending to her own needs rather than waiting for her husband to guess what she wanted. She resisted the belief that she deserved to have bad things happen. She used affirmations. She attended Adult Children of Alcoholics (ACOA) support group meetings.

Gradually and steadily, Mindy became less anxious, and her depression lessened. She came to the sessions with reports of a far more satisfying life. Then she left town for seven months, during which time I heard nothing from her.

When she returned, her story of family change amazed and delighted me. Her sons were now manageable, cooperative children. Her husband was able to share some of his own feelings and was looking at some of the pain from his own family of origin, although he had not yet attended ACOA meetings. Her mother had gone into therapy herself and had confronted Mindy's 22-year-old brother, who still lived at home and was abusing alcohol/other drugs. Mindy and her sister had been able for the first time to talk about the abuse they had suffered at their father's hands. Mindy had even had the courage to confront her father, tentatively but directly. Her mother, two aunts, and an uncle had talked together for the first time about the abuse in their family of origin, and one of her aunts had gone into therapy.

There is no way to know how much of this change was indirectly or directly related to the changes Mindy had chosen to make for herself. But it does seem very significant that Mindy, who was seen by her family of origin as the "strong one," was indeed strong enough to face her own shame-based feelings and identity — and the others followed.

"It's Too Easy"

We may find ourselves resisting change because it seems too simple. Trapped in the shame-anxiety cycle, we've been living lives of complex, tumultuous emotions and pain. It would seem that we need a complex plan or strategy to interrupt the cycle.

On the contrary: the 12-Step slogan "Keep It Simple" can be our guideline. We can concentrate on only one thing at a time. We can change only one part of ourselves at a time. Set a single goal for yourself — a simple one. Then give it lots of attention and time to work.

Many people come into therapy saying, "It's hopeless. I've tried everything." They may in fact have had some excellent ideas and tried virtually all of them. Probably they haven't tried any one of them for an extended period of time. Or they've tried several simultaneously without giving enough energy to any one.

You've probably heard the saying, "How can you drain the swamp when you're up to your neck in alligators?" Well, first we need to do something about the alligators. And we can only take care of the alligators one at a time. Start by trying to change a single thought, feeling, and behavior that has kept you mired in shame-anxiety. Don't worry if it seems "too easy." Eventually you will drain the swamp.

"You're not listening to me!" **Tyler's** voice rose as he confronted the group. "I don't give a rip if my neighbor smiles at me — especially if he's a guy. I want a girlfriend!"

The group members stood their ground as they told Tyler that he came across as too intense, too eager. Women would be scared off, they said, if he came on to them that way. The plan they had suggested — and to which Tyler was responding with such anger — was for him to start with a simple smile and greeting directed at his neighbors. He lived in a building with many senior citizens, a friendly bunch, and the group thought it would be a safe place for Tyler to practice. After listening to their point of view, he grudgingly agreed to try — "I guess so; what have I got to lose?"

They encouraged him week after week as he gained success and comfort, first with his neighbors, then with people out in the community. He reported how "the sales clerk seemed to like me — she smiled back!" And, "The cute girl who rides the bus with me said 'hello' to me first today."

The group rejoiced with him when he came in beaming because he had a date — with the granddaughter of one of his neighbors who had described him as "such a nice young man — so friendly!" By that time Tyler had made and maintained changes in his behavior affirming that he really was a "nice young man" — and also one who was moving out of his shame-based thinking.

The Whiplash Effect

As you begin to change, you may feel the "whiplash effect," a swinging pendulum of feelings that can be illustrated like this:

Stuck in a shame-based pattern   **Imagined ideal**

 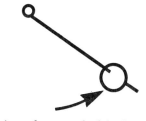

Life is horrible, rotten, awful, an endurance contest.   *Life is perfect, wonderful, always happy.*

Most people

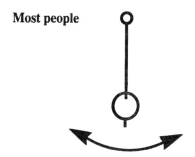

Life is a mixture of good, bad, and average.

When we are shame-based, our lives are stuck on one side of the pendulum's swing — the side of believing that we don't deserve good and do deserve bad. We have no idea that there's any other way to think or live. We have observed others who seem to live in less pain, but we don't know how they do it and we are angry about that.

When we take our first steps toward change, it's predictable that we will overreact and swing to the opposite side of the pendulum's arc. All the energy and force we have been using to hold on to our harmful or destructive shame-based beliefs will propel us toward the imagined ideal of a perfect, problem-free life. We will devote ourselves to "making it right." We may even find ourselves being compulsive about not being compulsive.

It takes time for a pendulum to stop swinging wildly and maintain a moderate arc in the middle. It will take time and practice for you to moderate to a middle ground of being the way you want to be. Up to now you have known only one way of being, an extreme. You will need to learn about other options, even those at the other extreme, before you can choose the one that works best and feels best for you.

Some people find it difficult to stay in the moderate swing of day-to-day life with its mixture of good, bad, and in-between. They are so accustomed to highs and lows that their new life seems bland and tasteless. They may even create crises just to add a little excitement (and return to a state that feels "natural" to them). If this happens to you, it doesn't mean that you're a failure. Nobody expects infants to start walking the first time they stand alone. Let yourself take a few "baby steps" — even if they're not always in the right direction.

The Inability to Play

Somehow we have come to accept that we must "work" on our personal growth, "work" on our healing, "work" on our relationships, "work" on our parenting, "work" on anything that has value to us. It's my personal position that the emphasis on "work" is tied directly to shame-anxiety and the shame-based belief that we don't deserve good. Our focus on work keeps us stuck in the shame-anxiety cycle.

I believe that play is one of humankind's most precious assets. Yet we consistently undervalue it. We justify the way our children spend their time by saying, "Play is the work of children." With today's pressure to create Superkids, there are many children who are pushed past "child's play" to structured play, exercise, and creative activities. Their intrinsic ability to play has been channeled into the "work" of growing up.

Certainly life is a serious business; as the old saying goes, "Not many of us make it out alive." But we've taken this seriousness too far. We plan our days, schedule our lives, keep ourselves busy and productive. We miss many chances not only to stop and smell the roses but also to spend a few minutes in conversation with a friend, cuddle with our loved ones, and in general be spontaneous. We get so caught up in busy-ness that we get pulled into the shame-anxiety cycle. In the intensity of "working our way through life," we have forgotten how to play.

When we stop and think about it, some of the richest times in our lives are when we are playing. Picture new parents with their baby: they coo, goo, and make funny faces. They smile with their child, they laugh together. Now think of how it was with your closest childhood friend. You giggled together over the opposite sex, laughed over your special jokes or secret words. Reflect back on when you and your love-mate first met. You played together, doing "silly" things like walking in the rain, touching each other when "your song" was playing, and making love. It was easy, wasn't it?

Some of us never learned how to play. We were caregivers for our siblings, sometimes for our parents. We grew up in caldrons of violence, alcoholism, mental illness, rigidity and shame. We adapted and accommodated in order to survive. The effects of that kind of upbringing are somewhat like having a permanently broken leg. We can adapt to the weight of the cast, adjust to the ongoing pain, keep moving despite the withered muscles in our immobilized leg. We can do what we have to do to survive. When we leave our childhood environment, the consequences are much like removing the cast. We can walk on the leg, but the long-term impairment has now created habits of movement that prevent us from walking naturally. We go through the motions, but we haven't learned how to do all the things people learn when they have freedom of movement.

When an infant is unable to engage in spontaneous smiling, cooing, and interactions with others, the condition is called "failure to thrive." Many adults have the same condition, but it is nameless.

Throughout this book, we have talked about many tools and techniques that can help to free you from the shame-anxiety cycle. Let's add a final, most significant one: the willingness to play, to be good to yourself, to allow yourself not the luxury but the necessity of play. When you play, you exercise your innate ability to see the absurdity of life, to relish the unexpected, to appreciate twists of humor and logic, to be able to laugh. So get serious about play! It will soon become easy, fun, spontaneous, zestful, energetic, and ultimately freeing.

THE COURAGE
TO HEAL

We gathered in a small chapel, 23 of us who had come together to join **Marea** in her "Passages Ceremony." She had come to a point in her shame healing where she wanted to use a ritual to symbolize letting go of her pain. She planned the ceremony carefully with a pastoral counselor who had been a significant support during the hard times of facing her memories and shame. Many of us participated in the reading of scripture, poetry, and reflections about what it had meant to us to be part of Marea's journey. It was a time of joyousness, a time of letting go, a time of celebrating the strength of the human spirit — of celebrating Marea.

It is difficult to convey in words the depth of feeling that we had experienced with Marea. I suspect it was difficult for any of us to know the extent of the gifts we had given her. For myself, I doubt that Marea can comprehend the gifts she has given me as she has allowed me to walk with her in the valley of fear of losing her very self, of standing in the radiance of hope, of seeing how her shame at once imprisoned her — and made it possible to set herself free.

Marea had survived profound sexual abuse beginning in her infancy. She had survived the loss of support from a mother who was unable to protect her. She had been physically, sexually, and psychologically abused by neighbors, relatives, a boyfriend. She had lost a foster daughter through suicide. But she had never lost the flicker of hope that she visualized as a tiny yellow dot deep within a being that she perceived as brown — the color of her feeling of being "dirt," the color of shame.

This is the poem Marea wrote about her healing:

Bear,
the cell?
the yellow cell of life?
do you remember?
the one buried and hidden deep within my
soul?

Bear,
that little cell
has
a
shape
now...
the cell
is
the little girl...
the child
of
ME...

It is an awesome journey, this business of setting out to change ourselves. It requires courage and fortitude. Shame provides the impetus to undertake this venture. Despite its apparently harmful consequences, shame is one of our most essential emotions. It expresses and affirms our humanity. And just as every problem or conflict contains the seed of an equivalent benefit or advantage, shame contains the seed of equivalent self-transformation.

Shame tells us that there is a higher state of being than the one we are in, a better and more fulfilling way to live. It alerts us that we have not yet achieved our best selves — and encourages us to try.

On days when you are warmed by the hope of healing, you may think that life will go on like this forever. It won't. There will be difficult times ahead, times when you feel the pull of old habits, old ways, old behaviors, old doubts and fears. This doesn't mean that your task is hopeless. It means that you're human.

I wish you a successful journey, full of surprises and joy.

MUTUAL HELP AND NETWORKING GROUPS

Alcoholics Anonymous (AA)
PO Box 459, Grand Central Station
New York, NY 10163
Telephone: (212) 686-1100

Al-Anon/Alateen Family Groups
PO Box 862, Midtown Station
New York, NY 10018-0862
Telephone: (212) 302-7240

Cocaine Anonymous (CA)
PO Box 1367
Culver City, CA 90232
Telephone: (213) 559-5833

Cocanon Family Groups
PO Box 1367
Culver City, CA 90232
Telephone: (213) 859-2206 or (212) 713-5133

Emotions Anonymous (EA)
International Service Group
PO Box 4245
St. Paul, MN 55104
Telephone: (612) 647-9712

Families Anonymous
PO Box 528
Van Nuys, CA 91408
Telephone: (818) 989-7841

Narcotics Anonymous (NA)
PO Box 9999
Van Nuys, CA 91409
Telephone: (818) 780-3951

Nar-Anon Family Groups
PO Box 9999
Van Nuys, CA 91409
Telephone: (213) 547-5800

National Association for Children of Alcoholics, Inc. (NACOA)
31582 Coast Highway, Suite B
South Laguna, CA 92677-3044
Telephone: (714) 499-3889

There are literally hundreds of mutual-support groups, many of them for chemically dependent people, many others for their friends and families. Some are quite specialized, such as groups for alcoholics with AIDS, or for adult children of alcoholic parents. A complete listing is beyond the scope of this book, but information is available from:

Self-Help Clearinghouse
Saint Clare's-Riverside Medical Center
Denville, NJ 07834
Telephone: (201) 625-7101, TDD (201) 625-9053
Compu Serve 70275,1003.

This clearinghouse publishes *The Self-Help Sourcebook*, which lists national offices for most groups that have them and can tell you how to find or, if need be, form local groups to meet almost any specific need.

FOR FURTHER READING

Al-Anon's Twelve Steps and Twelve Traditions (New York, NY: Al-Anon Family Group Headquarters, 1981.

The Twelve Steps: A Way Out (San Diego, CA: Recovery Publications, 1987).

Becker, Ernest, *The Denial of Death* (New York, NY: The Free Press, 1973).

Benson, Herbert, *The Relaxation Response* (New York, NY: Avon Books, 1975).

Black, Claudia, *Repeat After Me* (Denver, CO: Printing & Publications, 1985).

Bradshaw, John, *Bradshaw on the Family* (Deerfield Beach, FL: Health Communications, 1988).

Braiker, Harriet B., *The Type E Woman* (New York, NY: Dodd, Mead & Company, 1986).

Briggs, Dorothy Corkille, *Your Child's Self-Esteem* (New York, NY: Doubleday and Co., 1970).

Burns, David D., *Feeling Good* (New York, NY: New American Library, 1980).

Carnes, Patrick J., *Out of the Shadows* (Minneapolis, MN: CompCare Publications, Inc., 1984).

Cermak, Timmen L., M.D., *Diagnosing and Treating Co-Dependence* (Minneapolis, MN: Johnson Institute, 1986)— *A Time to Heal: The Road to Recovery for Adult Children of Alcoholics* (Los Angeles, CA: Jeremy P. Tarcher, Inc., 1988). Available from the Johnson Institute, 7151 Metro Boulevard, Minneapolis, MN 55435.

Damon, Janet, *Shopaholics* (Los Angeles, CA: Price Stern Sloan, 1988).

Daugherty, Lynn B., *Why Me?* (Racine, WI: Mother Courage Press, 1984).

Ferrucci, Piero, *What We May Be* (Los Angeles, CA: Jeremy P. Tarcher, Inc., 1982).

Fossum, Merle A. and Marilyn J. Mason, *Facing Shame: Families in Recovery* (New York, NY: W.W. Norton & Company, 1986). Available from the Johnson Institute, 7151 Metro Boulevard, Minneapolis, MN 55435.

Fromm, Erich, Ph.D., *The Ability to Love* (New York, NY: Harper & Row, 1956).

Gaylin, Willard, *Feelings: Our Vital Signs* (New York, NY: Harper & Row, 1979).

Gendlin, Eugene T., Ph.D., *Focusing* (New York, NY: Bantam, 1978).

Geringer-Woititz, Janet, Ed.D., *Struggle for Intimacy* (Pompano Beach, FL: Health Communications, Inc., 1985).

Gil, Eliana M., *Outgrowing the Pain* (Walnut Creek, CA: Launch Press, 1983).

Goldberg, Herbert, *The Hazards of Being Male* (New York, NY: Nash Publisher, 1976).

Gomberg, Edith S. Lisansky, "Shame and Guilt: Issues Among Women Alcoholics," *Counselor*, January-February 1989, pp. 23-24.

Johnson, Vernon E., D.D., *Intervention: How To Help Someone Who Doesn't Want Help* (Minneapolis, MN: Johnson Institute, 1986).

Jung, C.G., *Memories, Dreams, Reflections* (New York, NY: Vintage Books, 1961).

Jung, Carl S., ed., *Man and His Symbols* (Pine Brook, NJ: Dell Publishing Co., 1964).

Kaufman, Gershen, *Shame: The Power of Caring* (Cambridge, MA: Schenkman Publishing Company, Inc., 1980).

Kubler-Ross, Elisabeth, *On Death and Dying* (New York, NY: Macmillan, 1969).

Kurtz, Ernest, *Shame and Guilt* (Center City, MN: Hazelden, 1981).

Kushner, Harold, *When All You've Ever Wanted Isn't Enough* (New York, NY: Pocket Books, 1986).

Larsen, Earnie, *Stage II Recovery* (San Francisco, CA: Harper & Row, 1985).

Leonard, Linda Schierse, *The Wounded Woman* (Athens, OH: Swallow Press, 1982)

Lerner, Harriet Goldhor, *The Dance of Anger* (New York, NY: Harper & Row, 1985).

Lerner, Rokelle, *Daily Affirmations for Adult Children of Alcoholics* (Pompano Beach, FL: Health Communications, Inc., 1985).

Lewis, Helen B., *Shame and Guilt in Neurosis* (New York, NY: International Universities Press, 1971).

Lowen, Alexander, *Narcissism: Denial of the True Self* (New York, NY: Macmillan, 1985).

Lynd, Helen Merrell, *On Shame and the Search for Identity* (New York, NY: Harcourt, Brace & Company, 1958).

Maslow, Abraham H., *The Further Reaches of Human Nature* (New York, NY: Viking Press, 1971).

Mayer, Adele, *Sexual Abuse* (Holmes Beach, FL: Learning Publications, 1985).

Miller, Alice, *The Drama of the Gifted Child* (New York, NY: Basic Books, 1981).

Montagu, Ashley, *Touching* (New York, NY: Columbia University Press, 1971).

Morris, Herbert, ed., *Guilt and Shame* (Belmont, CA: Wadsworth Publishing Co., 1971).

Norwood, Robin, *Women Who Love Too Much* (New York, NY: Pocket Books, 1985).

Nouwen, Henri J.M., *The Wounded Healer* (Garden City, NJ: Doubleday & Company, 1979).

Patterson, Gerald R., *Families* (Champaign, IL: Research Press, 1971).

Piers, Gerhart and Milton B. Singer, *Shame and Guilt* (New York, NY: W.W. Norton & Company, 1971).

Peele, Stanton, Ph.D. and Archie Brodsky, *Love and Addiction* (New York, NY: New American Library, 1975).

Powell, John, *Why Am I Afraid to Love?* (Niles, IL: Argus Communications, 1972).

Rubin, Theodore Isaac, M.D., *The Angry Book* (New York, NY: Collier, 1970).
— *Compassion and Self-hate* (New York, NY: Collier Books/MacMillan, 1975).

Satir, Virginia, *Peoplemaking* (Palo Alto, CA: Science and Behavior Books, Inc., 1972).

Schaef, Anne Wilson, *Co-Dependence: Misunderstood — Mistreated* (San Francisco, CA: Harper & Row, 1986).— *When Society Becomes an Addict* (San Francisco, CA: Harper & Row, 1987).

Seixas, Judith and Geraldine Youcha, *Children of Alcoholism* (New York, NY: Harper & Row, 1983).

Skynner, Robin and John Cleese, *Families and How To Survive Them* (New York, NY: Oxford University Press, 1983).

Small, Jacquelyn, *Transformers* (Marina del Rey, CA: De Vorss and Company, 1982).

Stevens, John O., *Awareness: Exploring, experimenting, experiencing* (Moab, UT: Real People Press, 1971).

Stoddard, Alexandra, *Living a Beautiful life: 500 Ways to add Elegance, Order, Beauty, and Joy to Every Day of Your Life* (New York, NY: Random House, 1986).

Viorst, Judith, *Necessary Losses: The Loves, Illusions, Dependences, and Impossible Expectations that All of Us Have To Give Up in Order To Grow* (New York, NY: Fawcett Gold Medal, 1986).

Wegscheider-Cruse, Sharon, *Another Chance: Hope and Health for Alcoholic Families* (Palo Alto, CA: Science and Behavior Books, 1981).
— *Choice Making* (Pompano Beach, FL: Health Communications Inc., 1985).

Wholey, Dennis, *The Courage to Change* (Boston, MA: Houghton Mifflin Co., 1984).

Wilmes, David J., *Parenting for Prevention* (Minneapolis, MN: Johnson Institute, 1988).

Witkin, Georgia, *Quick Fixes and Small Comforts* (New York, NY: Villard Books, 1988).

Woititz, Janet, *Adult Children of Alcoholics* (Hollywood, FL: Health Communications, 1983).

Wurmser, Leon, *The Mask of Shame* (Baltimore, MD: Johns Hopkins University Press, 1981).

Zimmerman, Bill, *Make Beliefs* (New York, NY: Guarionex Press, 1987).

INDEX

A

B

Behavior
    as anxiety response, 59-61
    modification techniques, 68-70
Blaming self and others, anxiety and, 44
Boredom, as sign of anxiety, 136
Boundaries (self-others)
    defined, 24
    hypervigilance and, 48
    shame and, 25
    violations of, 26

C

Caffeine, anxiety and, 54-55
Caregivers, self-concept and, 29-30
Caretaking trap, avoidance of, 100-102
Catastrophizing, 109
Change, barriers to
    anticipation and, 133
    family loyalty and, 140-142
    fear of the new, 133-134
    inability to play, 144-145
    roadblocks, 133-145
    shame as force for, 7
    small increments of change, 62-63
    "too easy" excuse, 142-143
    "too late" excuse, 138-140, 139-140
    whiplash effect, 143-144
Chaos, anxiety and, 46-49
Chorus Line (musical), 32
Codependence, family loyalty and, 140-142
Cognitive distortion,
    "analysis paralysis," 113
    defined, 103-104
    grandiosity and, 118-119
    "I messages," 112
    identifying and changing, 108-113
    irrational thinking, 105-106
    judgmentalism, 106-107

D

E

F

G

H

I

N

O

P

V

W

JOHNSON INSTITUTE

When the Johnson Institute first opened its doors in 1966, few people knew or believed that alcoholism was a disease. Fewer still thought that anything could be done to help the chemically dependent person other than to wait for him or her to"hit bottom" and then pick up the pieces.

We've spent over twenty years spreading the good news that chemical dependence is a *treatable* disease. Through our publications, films, video and audiocassettes, and our training and consultation services, we've given hope and help to hundreds of thousands of people across the country and around the world. The intervention and treatment methods we've pioneered have restored shattered careers, healed relationships with co-workers and friends, saved lives, and brought families back together.

Today the Johnson Institute is an internationally recognized leader in the field of chemical dependence intervention, treatment, and recovery. Individuals, organizations, and businesses, large and small, rely on us to provide them with the tools they need. Schools, universities, hospitals, treatment centers, and other healthcare agencies look to us for experience, expertise, innovation, and results. With care, compassion, and commitment, we will continue to reach out to chemically dependent persons, their families, and the professionals who serve them.

To find out more about us, write or call:

7151 Metro Boulevard
Minneapolis, Mn 55435
1-800-231-5165
In MN: 1-800-247-0484
or 944-0511
In CAN: 1-800-447-6660

Need a copy for a friend? You may order directly.

UNDERSTANDING SHAME
Why It Hurts, How It Helps,
How You Can Use It to Transform Your Life

Eunice Cavanaugh, M.Ed., M.S.W.

Johnson Institute

$15.95

Order Form

Please send _____ copy (copies) of **UNDERSTANDING SHAME.** Price $15.95 per copy. Please add $3.00 shipping for the first book and $1.25 for each additional copy.

_____
Name (please print)

_____
Address

_____
City/State/Zip

_____
Attention

Please note that orders under $75.00 must be prepaid.
If paying by credit card, please
complete the following:

☐ Bill the full payment to my credit card.

☐ VISA ☐ MasterCard ☐ American Express

Credit card number: _____

For MASTERCARD
Write the 4 digits below the account number: _____

Expiration date: _____

Signature on card: _____

For faster service, call
our Order Department
TOLL-FREE:
1-800-231-5165
In Minnesota call:
1-800-247-0484
or **(612) 944-0511**
In Canada call:
1-800-447-6660

Return this order form to: The Johnson Institute
                               7151 Metro Boulevard
                               Minneapolis, MN 55435-3425
Ship to (if different from above):

_____
Name (please print)

_____
Address

_____
City/State/Zip

Need a copy for a friend? You may order directly.

UNDERSTANDING SHAME
Why It Hurts, How It Helps,
How You Can Use It to Transform Your Life
Eunice Cavanaugh, M.Ed., M.S.W.

Johnson Institute

$15.95

Order Form

Please send _____ copy (copies) of **UNDERSTANDING SHAME.** Price $15.95 per copy. Please add $3.00 shipping for the first book and $1.25 for each additional copy.

Name (please print)

Address

City/State/Zip

Attention

Please note that orders under $75.00 must be prepaid.
If paying by credit card, please
complete the following:

☐ Bill the full payment to my credit card.

☐ VISA ☐ MasterCard ☐ American Express

Credit card number: _____

For MASTERCARD
Write the 4 digits below the account number: _____

Expiration date: _____

Signature on card: _____

For faster service, call
our Order Department
TOLL-FREE:
1-800-231-5165
In Minnesota call:
1-800-247-0484
or **(612) 944-0511**
In Canada call:
1-800-447-6660

Return this order form to: The Johnson Institute
7151 Metro Boulevard
Minneapolis, MN 55435-3425
Ship to (if different from above):

Name (please print)

Address

City/State/Zip